The Voice of
GEN Z

Grace Masback

Dedicated to voiceless people everywhere

GRACE MASBACK aspires to give voice to the voiceless via journalism, community outreach, and advocacy. She holds the modest ambition of becoming the "Voice of Gen Z" and is the founder of *WANT*, a news, sports, and entertainment website that aggregates the best in high school journalism from school papers and teen bloggers worldwide (www.wantnewsforteens.com). Grace writes for the *Huffington Post* and *AwesomenessTV.com* and consults on web strategy and content for School of Doodle. She also heads up the Portland, Oregon-based firm, Voice of Gen Z Consulting (www.voiceofgenz.com). She lives by the C.G. Jung admonition, "You are what you do, not what you say you'll do."

Contents

Chapter 1

Introduction
How I became the Voice of Gen Z

I NEVER PLANNED to be the Voice of Gen Z. It just happened through a string of seemingly unrelated developments. I found my voice for the first time via a series of books I wrote with my father when I was little. Made of cardboard and bound with pipe cleaners, the first few were highly derivative of a popular children's book. The first was called, *Pat the Fluffygoat*. It was about a goat I liked at the Indianapolis Zoo. We "published" that when I was three. The next in the series was published when I was four. It was called *Pat the Lonely Goose* and was about a goose I had seen in a park. *Pat Shooter and Boots* came out a few months later. Things went off the rails a bit when I wrote *The Princess and Prince Book*, which told the story of a land where everyone was either a Princess or a Prince. My dad lost interest after that one and we never managed to finish the book about the time I lost a tooth on Christmas Eve, putting the tooth fairy and Santa Claus on a collision course. My nascent career as an author morphed into an assembly line of holiday-related books (Mother's Day,

Christmas, etc.) that I made as gifts for family members, who never seemed all that excited to receive them.

I first became conscious of my generation while creating my seventh grade science fair project. Because I was scared to death of "real" science, my project studied the apparel brand preferences of middle school girls. This was at the time when the Abercrombie moose was my god. And, why not — what teen wasn't attracted to the dark, heavily-perfumed, nightclub-like confines of the Abercrombie retail spaces, which just happened to feature muscled boys naked to the waist? At the time, I was happy that my place in society could be easily established by what shirt I wore or backpack I carried. Interestingly, my brand preference study revealed that other girls weren't quite so slavishly connected to the popular brands, hinting at a tectonic shift from previous generations. I began to notice how my peers differed from the Millennials just ahead of us.

My voice came to full flower when I started high school. I had transferred my loyalties from the moose to Taylor Swift, who I saw as the epitome of female style, talent, entrepreneurship, and empowerment. I was her target audience and had an idea that would allow me to combine my burgeoning interest in journalism with my fan-girl status. I wrote Ms. Swift proposing an interview focused on her positive messages for teen girls. At the same time, I went to my school paper and proposed that they print the interview. The school paper said freshmen couldn't be writers. Taylor Swift never responded.

Refusing to be disillusioned, I took matters into my own hands and launched *WANT*, a website that aggregates the best in high school journalism from school papers and teen bloggers worldwide (www.wantnewsforteens.com). We offer youth writers a platform and voice beyond the limited resources and readership of their school paper, providing youth a chance to cover big names and stories and compete with the adult-centric, mainstream media. *WANT* has partnered with school journalism programs and writers from Maine to Florida, New York to Hawaii, and several foreign countries – featuring content ranging from a discussion on the merits of college, to revolutionary art in Cuba, to the impending presidential election. *WANT's* immodest goal is to give voice to the voiceless, and to provide our peers with relevant news from their own perspective.

WANT gave me voice and a different kind of platform than that provided by the *Pat The Fluffygoat* book I created with my dad. It allowed me to tell my own stories. It allowed me to take a stand and share my perspective on myriad issues. WANT opened the door to the larger world of journalism, connecting me to a variety of different journalistic outlets. I began writing about issues of vibrant interest to my generation — everything from voting rights to Jon Stewart to the SAT.

This evolved, perhaps naturally, to writing about my generation, Generation Z. Gen Z is the generation of young people who have grown up in the shadows of our Millennial brothers and sisters, and we are currently struggling to define ourselves and claim our rightful place in the world. It's strange, the last thing I ever wanted to be was a cliche, someone who could be classified, labeled, lumped into a category and described en masse. But, the more I sensed that Gen Z was being marginalized and ignored, the more motivated I became to learn more about we stood for – I did research, I spoke with friends, and then I made an important decision – if no one else was going to speak up for Gen Z, I would. I would become the voice of Gen Z.

With that decision made, I began to write about Gen Z, for *Huffington Post* and other publications. This led to contacts with like-minded individuals around the country and a number of companies seeking insight into the Gen Z demographic. Sensing an opportunity, I formed Voice of Gen Z Consulting, Inc., a firm specializing in advising companies on how to connect to Gen Z. Building a staff of teens with interests similar to my own, I became an advocate for Gen Z and a resource for corporate America, also meeting my long-term objective of earning money to help pay for college. I now lead a network of other young people, working to help business and organizations fully understand our very complex, but increasingly powerful, generation.

No one could have predicted my journey to this moment. As a high school freshman, I was shy and voiceless. I lacked the confidence to pursue my ideas and share my perspective. Now I'm the voice of Gen Z. Go figure.

Chapter 2

Why Gen Z Matters
The Attributes that will make Gen Z America's next "Greatest Generation"

FOLLOWING A WARM and somewhat embarrassing introduction, I walk to the front of the room, survey the audience, and launch into my presentation. The screen features some baby pictures and a curvaceous woman clinging to a shiny pole:

Today is my 18th birthday. I am excited to enter the ranks of adulthood. I'm now legal to enter strip clubs, get a tattoo, buy cigarettes, and, if our political system doesn't implode on itself beforehand, vote in my first presidential election.

When I was growing up, my parents taught me two things. First, don't worry about what your future will look like — it will all be clear when you are grown up. And, second, just remember that no matter what happens, you can be anything you set your mind to.

While I can personally attest to the fact that my future doesn't seem any less murky now that I have turned 18, I believe wholeheartedly in the second piece of advice. I come from a generation brimming with passion and drive to be America's next "Greatest Generation" — to take the technology that surrounds us and use it to further society and change the world. I am a proud member of Generation Z.

Hi everyone. My name is Grace Masback and I am a high school senior from Portland, Oregon. I am all about giving voice to the voiceless, with the modest ambition of becoming the voice of my generation, Gen Z. I am passionate about journalism, politics and civic engagement, social justice advocacy, and criminal justice reform. But, everything I do comes back to my identity as a member of Generation Z.

The rest of the presentation was a pleasant blur. Once I got past the introduction part and established who I was, I felt confident in my ability to tell my story and that of my generation.

The occasion of that presentation was a summer 2016 summit put on by Navigate Research, a Chicago-based industry leader in evaluating and measuring marketing investments, primarily in sports and entertainment. I became linked to them earlier in the year after their Founder and President, AJ Maestas, heard about my seventh grade science project that I described briefly above. Back in those days I hated science, and when I was told that every student was required to do a science fair project, I picked the most non-sciency project I could think of, one consistent with being a brand-obsessed teen — "An Analysis of the Brand Preferences and Purchase Decisions of Middle School

Girls." To my chagrin, I actually ended up winning an award at both my regional and state science fairs, extending my time as a science geek. Still, the project sparked my passion for research and reinforced my interest in the topic of brand preference. AJ Maestas had the novel idea that my passion for cracking the code of brand preferences combined with my insights into Gen Z gleaned from my work with *WANT* would be of interest to Navigate and some of its clients.

Navigate became one of the first clients of Voice of Gen Z Consulting, a business concept I conceived of a couple of years ago. I work with the Navigate team to provide insight into the patterns of behavior and preferences of my generation. I do this by offering a combination of my inherent knowledge, conversations with my peers, surveys, literature reviews, and data analysis. The Navigate team pushes me (and, indirectly, my network) to tap into the rich veins of insight about the country's fastest growing generation in order to mine the data that will be valuable to them and their partners.

My writing and the work I do for Navigate and other clients has me excited about being a voice for and conduit to a group of young people whose potential, until recently, has been ignored. The being ignored point agitates and highly motivates me. I see inter-generational history repeating itself and don't like it. From what I've seen, Baby Boomers still play an out-sized role in society, dominating Gen X, Millennials, and Gen Z. I find it almost comical that the boys in my class listen to Jimi Hendrix and Led Zeppelin, often instead of music from my era. That would be like my dad, who was born in 1955, listening to Benny Goodman and Bix Beiderbecke, stars of the 1920s and 1930s, instead of Janis Joplin and the Allman Brothers. Do we really need to see another documentary about The Beatles? The existence (and success) of "classic rock" radio stations is more related to the ongoing hegemony of the Baby Boomer generation than it is the intrinsic superiority of the music played (though I admit that I like some of my father's favorite music).

Similarly, Millennials, who precede Gen Z in the generational lineup, are exercising incredible influence on society today, through companies they've founded, such as Facebook and Snapchat, the articles they write, the fashions they design, and the money they spend. I respect the fact that they are the worker bees of societal enterprise and I admire much of their creative impact – they ushered global society from one millennium to the next and accelerated the flattening of the world.

That said, they are relentlessly pessimistic (the Great Recession hit them hard) and dangerously detached from much of the reality of what the world is facing. I like the Lewis Black description of Millennials, "swarming the USA and leaving nothing but selfie-sticks and gluten-free pizza crusts in their wake." The fact that many Millennials flocked to Gary Johnson without even knowing what he stood for, even though supporting Johnson might facilitate the election of Donald Trump, told me everything I needed to know about the depth of their political convictions. When I make presentations or write articles, I'm often advised to tone down my criticism of Millennials as they often are the predominate audience for my work, but to quote Mark Cuban, of *Shark Tank* and the Dallas Mavericks fame, "It's time for the Millennials to relinquish their throne – Gen Z will have their own unique spin on the future."

While it's true that many in my generation are still inexperienced and oblivious to the intricacies of the world around us, we are curious, passionate, creative, full of energy, and in the words of Kristen Kelley, the CMO of Randstad, Gen Z is "hyperoptimistic," a stark contrast to Millennials. Not incidentally, Gen Z possesses $44 billion in direct spending power and $500 billion in influence over our parents' purchase decisions. To me, we are the antidote to the detachment and negativity of the Millennial generation and it irks me when the hegemony exercised by what I call the "MIC" – the Millennial Industrial Complex – overwhelms and silences my generation.

So, who is Gen Z? Although I can draw on my own 18 years of personal fieldwork, I've also looked closely at my peers and have conducted comprehensive research in academic literature and the marketing world's leading publications. Gen Z, also known as "Gen I," "Gen Next," "Centennials," "Pluralists," "Founders," or "iGeneration," is the group of young people born between the late 1990s and the early 2000s. I am on the edge of this divide, with my senior class, the high school class of 2017, roughly representing the boundary between Gen Z and our predecessors the Millennials (some would call the high school classes of either 2015 or 2016 the dividing line). According to the Pew Research Center, there are 82 million members of Gen Z, with 93 percent of Gen Z members having a real say in the family purchasing decisions I mention above.

Social researcher Mark McCrindle says Gen Z is the "most connected, educated, and sophisticated generation in history." In reference to Gen Z, he says, "They don't just represent the future, they are creating it." We are the first generation of true tech natives, meaning that we've grown up in a world of complex technology and the internet – a fully-functioning internet has existed our entire lifetime and the iPhone was launched when we were just starting school. As tech natives, we have a unique relationship with technology that allows us to use it productively and effectively instead of floundering under its potential. We are smart, self-directed, self-aware, innovative, goal oriented — and exceedingly modest. According to the "Cassandra Report," 89 percent of us spend our free time doing productive activities instead of just hanging out.

Unlike some previous generations, our parents are less likely to shelter and protect us, encouraging us to encounter the dangers and imperfections of the world. After all, we were around 10 years old when the Great Recession hit. We recognize the world's problems, including reduced opportunities in the traditional economy, so we are becoming our own bosses, starting for-profit and nonprofit companies at rates unheard of in any other generation. According to a recent Ernst & Young report, 63 percent of Gen Z members aspire to start their own company one day.

We have a level of interest in and commitment to our communities that exceeds that of all previous generations. Part of this has been hard-wired by our parents and schools, as most schools now require that we do "community service" in some form. While as a teenager my knee jerk reaction is to reject something I am told to do, making community service obligatory means that there are ubiquitous and meaningful ways for us to impact our communities and communities around the world. Gen Z embraces the experiential learning that comes from our outreach to and involvement in the world.

Interestingly and perhaps in response to the polarizing nature of the political climate in which we've been raised, we are aggressively non-partisan as a generation. Our engagement is with the world and its future, *our* future, not with a particular political party or movement. Granted, our close to unanimous opinion that global warming is real and requires urgent action by governments and industry, does implicate what passes for a "debate" on the American political scene, but no serious person denies the existence of the peril posed by global warming. Our goal is to work for causes and support initiatives that address society's problems, irrespective of the methodology of achieving a positive outcome. We are outcome oriented and support government and market solutions, and don't place a value on one over the other.

Additionally, according to studies conducted by the *New York Times* and others, Gen Z is more tolerant and open-minded than any previous generation. We matured and live in a world where sticking to the socially constructed binary is no longer the norm and where gender fluidity and racial diversity, tolerance, and acceptance are celebrated. I've termed us the first "post-race," "post-gender" generation. Not surprisingly, some see us as overly politically correct, and for the many positive attributes I identify with

Gen Z, this may be one area where we are on the precipice of taking things too far.

So, I'm pretty bullish about my generation, and believe in its potential. With that in mind, I aim for this book to help you understand what my generation is all about, what it is looking for in life, and how those interested in working with and selling to Gen Z can do so. The chapters that follow look to systematically define our key characteristics, including our relationship to technology (Chapter 3), our entrepreneurial spirit (Chapter 4), our community consciousness (Chapter 5), our non-partisan but pro-world approach (Chapter 6), our thirst for experiential learning (Chapter 7), and our unique and evolving race and gender profile (Chapter 8). I will also offer some specific views on how to connect to Gen Z (Chapter 9) and a concluding chapter that identifies how Gen Z will be our next "Greatest Generation," my hope being that this status can be achieved without the need to prove our greatness during a world war as was the case for the generation that preceded the Baby Boomers (Chapter 10). At the end of the chapters, you'll find a profile of someone who exemplifies the Gen Z spirit related to each of the topics. It's an additional way to get inside the psyche of Gen Z and to better understand what's motivating this amazing generation.

There is nothing particularly objective or balanced about this book – I am a Gen Z advocate and enthusiast. But, I hope you will share my view that my descriptions of the attributes and potential of Gen Z are accurate and compelling, and that the future of our country and world will be in safe hands.

Chapter 3
Gen Z as Technology Natives

WHEN THE WORDS "teen" and "social-media" are uttered together, for the majority of the American public a clear image comes to mind. A young person sits or stands, hunched over a small bright screen, furiously tapping, taking selfies, inserting the appropriate emojis. A recent article by *WIRED Magazine* served to reinforce this image. The author embedded herself in the lives of five teens from across the country as a means of understanding and writing about their social media habits. The ultimate message of the article was all-too-familiar. It painted a picture of technology-obsessed young people, constantly glued to smartphones and computer screens, allowing their lives to be controlled by a contrived set of rules and social norms that dictate how they communicate, with whom they talk, and how they view the world.

While I would like to dismiss the article as a generational cliché — something that twists the full truth about the role of tech in the lives of Gen Z — the reality is that tech and social media *do* play a role in some way in the lives of nearly all teens today. One commentator noted that Gen Z is always connected to a near seamless cloud-based world of friends, data, and entertainment. We send texts at twice the rate of Millennials. Whether they are "popular," anti-social, nerdy, or jocks, social media permeates everyone's life. As Dan Schawbel has observed, technology is like oxygen to Gen Z, fueling everything we do, including 66 percent of us who say that technology makes them feel that anything is possible.

The key to understanding Gen Z is that we've taken the notoriously short attention span of Millennials and reduced it further, not because we can't dive deep into topics, but because as technology or digital "natives" we've spent our whole lives training to engage with the constantly changing technology landscape, and can process digital content with amazing speed. In the words of Jeff Fromm of Futurecast the impact of Gen Z is significant because, "Technology advances culture at warp speed."

Imagine the terror of companies trying to figure out how to connect to Gen Z when we have an eight-second attention span (or less). As Jason Dorsey, the co-founder of the Center for Generational Kinetics, observes, "Gen Z likes messaging apps that don't leave a paper trail" – apps that permit instantaneous communications, that disappear quickly, and that allow the user to move on to the next form of communication. Bill Carter, a top expert on youth marketing, summarized the Gen Z view of the Tech World:

Facebook – *for parents posting pictures of their kids*
Tumblr – *for fandom of music, games, and movies*
Twitter – *it's fun to Tweet at events*
Snapchat – *where I brag and post selfies*

Pinterest – *it's for people who knit*
Instagram – *what everyone uses*

The 2016 Piper Jaffray "Taking Stock With Teens" report reinforces this, noting that 80 percent of teens use Snapchat, about the same as Instagram (79 percent), but only 52 percent of teens use Facebook (a number that falls to 30 percent for 14-year-olds). The *WIRED* article agrees, stating that Snapchat and Instagram are, by far, the most popular social channels among Gen Z, while Twitter, Facebook, and Kik are increasingly ignored (never mind poor Pinterest).

Julie Ginches, the CMO of Kahuna, calls Gen Z the "first truly mobile-only generation." When thinking about Gen Z, remember that the first iPhone came out when we were in third grade and the younger edge of the Gen Z cohort was handed an iPad as a toddler. Not surprisingly, a recent survey found that Gen Z sees age 13 as the appropriate age for kids to get their first smartphone, whereas Millennials, Gen X, and Baby Boomers see age 18 as the more appropriate age. We've heard about, but never experienced, dial-up, and take high speed internet for granted. In fact, one study indicates that 90 percent of Gen Z would be upset if they had to give up their internet connection, while only 50 percent would be upset to give up going out for dinner.

Given that technology has been part of our lives since we were kids, we don't just engage with technology, we actively shape it. To the extent that tech does play an outsized role in our lives, Gen Z is caught in a crosscurrent of different influences. We may not read printed newspapers or watch network news shows, but we are finding our own way to follow current events and engage with the world using social media. About 30 percent of our information comes from peers via social media. We engage in little or no "appointment watching" of television. We watch less than one hour of television a day, and a Wildness, Inc. study says 0% of Gen Z consider their television their "most important device." We do embrace NetFlix and are the dominant consumer of YouTube videos (watching an average of four hours per day). If our Millennial predecessors were more materially oriented than us and launched on-line buying, we savor "experiences" over shiny objects but have embraced buying via our mobile devices. So, we do many of the same things that previous generations have done, we just do them in different ways.

Social media clearly delivers both positive and negative effects. On the positive side, studies report that Gen Z finds social media an empowering tool that has resulted in an unprecedented degree of connectivity among its cohort. The downsides of our engagement with social media are all too clear – cyberbullying and sexist attacks on young girls to name a couple. Jason Dorsey observes that 42 percent of Gen Z say that social media has a direct impact on how they feel about themselves, with a negative impact on self-worth commonplace.

That said, I'm going to take a slightly contrarian point-of-view and say that for many kids social media does NOT play a dominant role — it is *not* an obsession, it is not something that is thought about on a 24/7 basis, there is no ongoing, thoughtful curation of photos, there is no constant and uber careful consideration of social norms. Social media is just something that they have because everyone else has it. Most young people are living presently in the world, using social media simply as a way to *supplement* their existence and capture memories. While 83 percent of Gen Z owns a Smartphone, my cohorts want to use technology to enhance their lives, not to be dominated by technology. As Sam Paschel of Skullcandy says, "Generation Z relates to technology as a tool, as opposed to an obsession."

Using my own school as a microcosm for the behavior of teens in society-at-large (my statistics teacher would probably not approve), the breakdown is clear. There are the teens obsessed with their social life. For them, socializing is their eighth class. These are the young people most likely to be glued to their phones, obsessing over Snapchat "streaks," and deleting old Instagram photos. Then, there are those who use social media only occasionally. They see it as a fun way to catch up with old friends or share snippets of their lives. They still care about their social media presence, but they aren't overly concerned about it. Finally, there are those who have social media but rarely use it. For them, social media is simply another way to connect with their closest friends, and they use it selectively. This breakdown in mind, using the first group to make generalizations about teens as a whole (the *WIRED* article) is both wrong and alarming.

Despite Gen Z's actual accomplishments and potential, adults are falling prey to the perception that young people are silly and worthless based on articles that take Gen Z's tech savvy and conflate it into an unhealthy, superficial obsession, glossing over attributes deserving of respect and appreciation. Yes, the teenagers of today are the first generation of true tech natives and technology will continue to play an important role in our lives and existence. At the same time, young people are so much more than the technology they use and the choices they make with it. The *WIRED* article illustrates an extreme, but the whole picture is much more complex.

Technology Native Profile – Hannah Scott

Hannah Scott, a high school senior from Los Angeles, California, is known as "code girl." She loves creating things with code and looks forward to exploring coding further. However, she is not your everyday computer geek — she is creative, a leader, and a woman. She fell in love with technology when she took a robotics class her sophomore year, and since then has combined this passion with her desire to help others by founding *To Infinity and Beyond*, an after-school science, technology, engineering, and mathematics program that strives to maximize the potential of disadvantaged youth in South Central Los Angeles.

What is your earliest memory involving technology?

I'm not exactly sure, but I know my mom has pictures of me sitting in front of a computer playing Webkinz and Club Penguin — I was obsessed. My brother also used to get tons of LEGOs for his birthday and Christmas, but he never liked playing with them. Instead, I would spend hours sprawled on the floor of my brother's room assembling pirate ships and Millenium Falcons.

How has technology evolved and changed over the course of your lifetime?

Personally, technology has transformed from an obscure thing that I would never understand to both a means of self-expression and an avenue for social change.

Today, how do you meld technology use into your daily life?

Aside from my app development job and my computer sciences classes at school, I use social media (Instagram, Twitter, Snapchat, Facebook) every day because I see it as a vehicle for both self-expression, self-love, and activism.

What role has technology played in your education and extracurricular activities?

Unfortunately, my (all-girls) school does not have a very strong computer science program — the only tech-related class we have is a Robotics course. Taking that class sparked my curiosity and fascination, and I had to learn everything I could about coding. So, last year, my school gave me an independent study block to teach myself how to code, and I did! Equipped with a new arsenal of self-taught programming languages, I took a job with *School of Doodle*, an online platform that encourages teen girls to assert their creative confidence, working on a top-secret tech project that will be announced soon!

How do you reconcile an interest in STEM with a passion for journalism and creatively telling stories?

I've been a creative person my whole life, which I've expressed through concert photography and writing. So, when I had that fateful encounter with coding sophomore year, I subconsciously doubted that my creative side would show because of that internalized perception of a computer programmer. I pictured a white teenage boy, wearing a hoodie, spending hours alone in his basement, fueled by Red Bull, hammering away at his computer keyboard in order to hack into some database. After taking a job at *School of Doodle* that combined coding and writing, I soon learned that creativity is absolutely fundamental to computer science, and it made me fall in love with coding in the first place. Sometimes, the utter lack of restriction and guidance in coding made me feel lost at sea without a compass, trying desperately not to throw my computer overboard. But, this utter lack of restriction and guidance is actually where my creative juices shine, whether I am designing the user experience and graphics that make an app both intuitive and aesthetically pleasing or writing algorithms that handle user chat rooms and image uploading.

Why is STEM education so important?

I believe STEM education is important because basic

scientific and technological principles empower students to think differently and take a new approach to problem solving. One of the things I teach my students in *To Infinity and Beyond* is computational thinking, which is the approach computer scientists take to problem-solving. The four steps are: (1) break the big problem into smaller pieces, (2) look for patterns between the problems, (3) abstract the smaller details that make the problems differ from each other, and (4) find a solution and write down the steps you took to get there. This problem-solving method and many other STEM principles can be applied to any other field of study and to our daily lives.

What have you done to promote STEM education?

I created *To Infinity and Beyond*, a weekly science, technology, engineering, and mathematics program that strives to expand the potential of South Central Los Angeles youth. The goal of this program is to inspire students who lack access to STEM education to pursue a career in the scientific and technological fields, and show them that programmers and rockets scientists can look like anyone — including themselves. My brilliant students have programmed LEGO robots, launched bottle rockets, coded their own visual storybooks, and created sales pitches for their own inventions.

If your house was burning and you could only save one piece of technology what would it be?

My record player/receiver/speakers — it took me a lot of time and MacGyvering to achieve the perfect setup, and I'm a sucker for the nostalgia and aesthetic appeal of listening to music on vinyl.

What do you see for the future of technology?

In the future, the gap between humanity and technology will narrow. This is not to say that the robots will take over and makes humans their slaves, so don't sound the alarm. Instead, when we are able to make our technology more human, we will be able to help more people and solve more global issues. Additionally, the influx of more women and people of color into the tech field, thus adding more diverse perspectives to the creators of tech, will engender new technological approaches to problems affecting people all over the world.

What do you see in your future?

In the future, I see myself pioneering the next greatest development at a startup or tech company before I go on to found and lead my own company that uses technology to empower others (not sure what that will be quite yet!). I hope to serve as a role model for other young girls interested in technology, and encourage them to pursue a career in technology.

Chapter 4

Gen Z:
The Entrepreneurial Generation

IT WAS A DARK, cold Friday afternoon in February. A gaggle of a hundred high school kids, mostly boys, paced nervously around the meeting space as the time for the meeting approached. Most were dressed in jeans and black t-shirts, many of which touted the merits of obscure punk rock bands. The first session of start-up weekend was about to begin. Meredith Goddard, the weekend's organizer, asked everyone to take a seat. She explained the ground rules for the weekend. Anyone with an idea for a new business would have one minute to pitch it to the group. After the pitches, the students would choose the 10 best concepts. Then, the students behind each of the winning concepts would have 30 minutes to recruit a staff to help develop their concept over the next 48 hours. Sunday evening, the ten new businesses would have five minutes to present their concept to a panel of judges. A winning business would get an all-expenses paid trip to California to visit SpaceX and meet Elon Musk.

Forty students chose to pitch ideas. The pitches ranged

from deeply serious and super technical to amusing and easy to understand. One student proposed a device that could produce cookies in the shape of an ice cream cone, allowing you to enjoy two treats at the same time. Another pitched the creation of a new kind of ad agency that would crowd-source ads for clients (like Taco Bell has done for Super Bowl commercials). A third pitched an app that notified you when it was time to take medications, and notified a third party if you failed to acknowledge receiving the notice. While their presentation skills varied, the passion behind all of the ideas was infectious. Everyone was imbued with a sense of the possible.

Start-up weekends or similar programs have become commonplace across the United States, responding to an interest among Gen Z teens to use their creativity and easy access to information and technology to emulate the most significant revolutionary forces of their childhood – giant names like Steve Jobs, Elon Musk, and Mark Zuckerberg, and lesser-known, but still important entrepreneurs like Brian Chesky and Joe Gebbia of Airbnb or Tim Westergren of Pandora. If earlier generations looked up to groundbreak-ers in music (The Beatles), or sports (Muhammed Ali), or politics (Dr. Martin Luther King, Jr.), ours has role models in the form of business people who created massive businesses with lightening speed. People who took simple insights and leveraged them into society-changing movements.

As noted above, Gen Z is a group of self-starters, with one Gallup study indicating that eight in 10 students in fifth through eighth grade want to be their own boss one day. An entrepreneur.com article confirms that high school students today want to start their own business – aiming to be "pioneers" not "career settlers." A Northeastern University study of 16 to 19 year olds found that 63 percent wanted to learn about entrepreneurship in college, including how to start their own business. Fueled by social media and enabled by apps and easy access to information of every kind, members of Gen Z share ideas and quickly turn notions into businesses. The trend has been encouraged by the consistently difficult financial circumstances throughout their childhood and the disappearance of a lot of the part-time, low-wage jobs that traditionally employed teens.

My own exposure to Gen Z entrepreneurship began at a start-up weekend and grew apace. It was at such an event that *WANT*, my news, sports, and entertainment website, was launched. In a moment of personal courage, I got up in front of over 100 people to pitch my idea, and I was surprised when my idea for creating "the world's first global, on-line, school newspaper" was chosen as one of the 10 ideas. The next 48 hours zipped by as we chose a name (Web-Accessible-News for-Teens/*WANT*), created the site, designed a logo, did a couple of rounds of customer validation, secured content from high school papers, sourced a couple of original articles, sold ads, and prepared for our final presentation.

We ended up "losing," as the concept for the student-run ad agency that crowdsourced its creative concepts won the top prize, but we did win the prize for "Best Customer Validation," which excited us, and one of the judges offered me a job after the event. What struck me most was the passion, engagement, and creativity of my fellow students. All of us were busy with school and other extra-curricular activities – sports teams, Mock Trial, robotics, Model U.N., community service activities, part-time jobs, and many other pursuits. But for this 48 hours, we all focused on entrepreneurship, and everyone discovered that they had something to offer. That last point was my most important take-away from the start-up weekend – raised in an environment in which entrepreneurship and innovation were celebrated, coming of age at a time when *Shark Tank* and similar shows were ubiquitous, we'd internalized many of the skills necessary to be a good entrepreneurs.

And, we weren't some isolated group of kids. The focus on entrepreneurship is common across America. In fact, if you are looking for what may be the best reason why Gen Z will be America's next "Greatest Generation," go no further than our comparative advantage vis-à-vis the rest of the world when it comes to youth entrepreneurship. True, the kids in Shanghai and Singapore may beat us on math tests – you hear lots of gloom and doom about American kids slipping behind academically – but no country's youth boasts a better combination of tech savvy, creative bravado, and natural marketing know-how. There may be areas where America has lost its mojo, entrepreneurship is not one of them.

Among the skills that are commonplace among Gen Z that support this entrepreneurial bent are a quick tendency to collaborate, a willingness to set lofty (even naïve) goals, the ability to work in a flat organization, and a readiness to commit to the focus necessary to see a project through to fruition. The media is full of stories of Gen Z entrepreneurs, such as 17-year-old Connor Blakely, who was recently pro-filed by *Forbes*. Blakely is a lifelong entrepreneur, having launched a homework-selling network when he was 14. The Ohio native works with a Canadian-based brand advisory company, the Intercept Group, and heads up a youth marketing publication, *YouthLogix*. While attending a recent Genius Network meeting, Blakely went through an exercise that confirmed to him that "having a 'why'" is the key to entrepreneurial success as it keeps you focused and committed and open to ongoing learning. A proud member of Gen Z, he brags, "Gen Z is the first generation that can take a selfie, order a pizza, and FaceTime their friend all at the same time."

I had the opportunity to meet an incredible group of Gen Z entrepreneurs when I made a presentation to one local program, TYE Oregon, which is linked to efforts in 23 cities around the world and seeks to encourage students to become the next generation of entrepreneurs and business leaders. The TYE group was hyper- attentive to my description of my own entrepreneurial journey and some of them later shared their own big ideas with me. At TYE, businessmen mentors coach high school students over a seven-month period based on a business-focused curriculum. The program participants are introduced to entrepreneurship, encouraged to ideate, work in teams to develop their concepts, and then compete for a trip to a global final. The emphasis of the program is to expose budding entrepreneurs to the attention to detail and due diligence needed to succeed, the basic business skills required to start a venture, the need for a brand positioning statement, the art of the sale, the sources of seed funding, and the keys to leadership and teamwork.

While I didn't have any TYE-like formal coaching as I tried to take *WANT* to the next level, I benefitted from an entire network of mentors, ranging from teachers at my school, to local business leaders, to family friends. Later, we applied to be part of the Portland Incubator Experiment (PIE), a start-up incubator operated by the global ad agency, Wieden & Kennedy, telling the story of the *WANT* team via a black and white video that mimicked The Beatles "A Hard Day's Night." We were one of nine start-ups selected from more than 400 applicants and spent several months working with the PIE team and Wieden & Kennedy branding experts. They designed a logo for *WANT*, helped us better define our brand and what we stood for, and helped us network in the local and national start-up community. We were also contacted by a Silicon Valley venture capitalist and traveled to Sand Hill Road for a meeting. Though we didn't attract any VC or angel funding, we learned a lot from the conversations about how to improve *WANT* and expand its impact, including launching a *WANT*-inspired initiative, the Voice of Gen Z Consulting firm.

One of the defining differences of Gen Z is that an independently-minded, creative interest in creating a business opportunity instead of going to work in a traditional job is commonplace among today's teens. It may be that this bit of Gen Z bravado will be short-lived and a passing fad, but no previous generation has ever been so confident in its ability to create its own career opportunities and then gone out and done so.

Gen Z Entrepreneur Profile: Michael Ioffe

Michael Ioffe is a high school senior at Lincoln High School in Portland, Oregon. From a young age he has believed in the power and influence of young people to make a difference in the world. A serial entrepreneur, he takes an action-oriented approach to life, whether it be launching a groundbreaking speaker series or leading his fellow students in a school walk-out to protest the Portland School Board's failure to address key issues facing high school students today.

At what age did you recognize your entrepreneurial spirit and what was your first experience with the world of entrepreneurship?

Very early on. I published and sold my first book in fourth grade, and quickly realized the power of making cool, innovative things and selling them. I was really into publishing for a while, and my first three books — all anthologies — sold a total of about a hundred copies. That changed my perception of what I was capable of doing.

What tools and resources have you taken advantage of as you have attempted to navigate the world of entrepreneurship?

Reaching out to business and non-profit leaders that I admire has helped me understand and navigate the world of entrepreneurship. Learning from these individuals has aided me in both my personal and professional development.

What organizations and companies have you founded?

I founded the Stumptown Speaker Series, a series of free business, leadership, and entrepreneurship talks in Portland. I later founded TILE, an organization that expanded the Stumptown model to ten cities internationally. We are currently growing at a rate of one new location per week. I also started the #FlockPPS movement, which is a unified student initiative to fight for more transparency and equality at Portland Public Schools.

Have your different initiatives been successful?

Stumptown, TILE, and #FlockPPS have all been very successful. Stumptown is now one of Portland's largest educational resources for students interested in business, leadership, and entrepreneurship, and TILE is on it's way to becoming a meaningful educational resource globally. #FlockPPS' recent protest has received national media attention and has made progress in changing how the Portland school district operates.

Why are entrepreneurial skills so valuable in today's world?

Entrepreneurial skills foster vision and ambition while pushing for meaningful action to fulfill a goal. They are vital in any field — not just business. The synthesis of vision, ambition, and action becomes more important as a skill set as we deal with increasingly complex global issues.

What is inspiring so many young people to engage in entrepreneurship?

I would say access to tools and resources. With enough hard work and determination, anyone now has the power to create what they want.

What has it been like to be a young entrepreneur? What lessons have you learned? What challenges have you faced?

It's been fun. I am very lucky to have a fantastic support system. I've learned that very few people have both the right vision and the right execution — proper execution matters a lot. I've faced a variety of challenges, but none that significantly impact my ability to move forward.

What do you want to do next? What are your goals for the future?

I'm passionate about affordable housing. Pursuing that from an entrepreneurial perspective seems like the logical next step for me after college.

Chapter 5

Gen Z's Community Consciousness

THE COMMUNICARE CLUB MEETING was called to order. On today's agenda was the question of which charitable category would be the beneficiary of the funds we'd raised this year. The first speaker advocated for the disabled, arguing passionately that recent school budget cutbacks had, inevitably, reduced services to disabled students. I suggested funding immigrant-related nonprofits. While my hometown wasn't a huge magnet for immigrants, the services to help newly arrived immigrants function and assimilate were underdeveloped and under-resourced. After a healthy discussion, we concluded that we'd focus on immigrants this year.

CommuniCare exemplifies a defining characteristic of Gen Z, the first generation for which community service is the norm not the exception. For generations, school, faith-based, and other community organizations have given empathetic and motivated young people the chance to contribute to their community and world. While some kids chose to participate, most did not. Beginning with the Millennials, required community service became the norm at most high schools. "Service" became a burden or obligation for most students, with their experience often a shallow one that wasn't very impactful for either the students or the recipients of their assistance. While many schools still require community service, the programs are versions 2.0 or 3.0, structured in such a way that students are more meaningfully engaged, make a significant contribution, and see a pathway to longer term, deeper involvement in the issue or charity.

The CommuniCare program takes students on a journey that touches the entire ecosystem of philanthropic work. First, the students engage in traditional fund-raising, everything from bake sales, to raffles, to school dances or other social events. A local foundation, the Harold & Arlene Schnitzer CARE Foundation, matches what the students raise 10 to 1, meaning that raising $1000 results in a fund of $11,000 to allocate. Next, the students discuss what charitable activity best addresses their critical concerns, hence the debate described above about whether to support charities helping the disabled or immigrants. Once the charitable activity is chosen, the CommuniCare Club invites organizations working in that area to make grant proposals. After reviewing the proposals and interviewing the groups, the Club allocates the funds to different organizations.

The genuine Gen Z commitment to community service may be an outgrowth of the alarming trend toward a sharply divided American society. Many political and social commentators focus on the economic divide between the "1%" and the rest of the country, or on the group of white males who feel themselves losing their traditional position of power in society. But, as members of Gen Z we are experiencing a divide in real time that runs far deeper than any described on the front page of newspapers or landing pages of websites. It's a broader socio-economic divide between the "haves" and the "have nots," the features of which exacerbate, enhance, and widen the divide further. The "haves" have higher incomes, easy access to good educational institutions, healthcare, a good diet, an environment that encourages physical activity, and other resources that message to them about the importance of maintaining a healthy lifestyle. The "have nots" are poor and have little access to a good education, bad healthcare options, bad diets, limited options for physical activity, and an environment in which sedentary lifestyles and obesity are increasingly the norm. Many members of Gen Z see these trends and realize that their futures will be harmed if this divide is allowed to continue to grow.

Among the other notable programs encouraging community service and outreach in the Gen Z demographic is the ANNpower Vital Voices Initiative, a program of ANN Inc., the parent company of Ann Taylor and LOFT, and the Vital Voices Global Partnership, a global nonprofit that works with women leaders in the areas of economic empowerment, political participation, and human rights. Each year, the ANNpower Vital Voices program selects 50 high school sophomore and junior girls to become ANNpower Fellows. The initiative aims to give these young women the leadership skills needed to have immediate and long-term impact on their communities.

In addition, the initiative supports innovative projects that bring about positive social change. Among the ventures supported are: (1) the Pink Portrait Project, which supports and celebrates women impacted by breast cancer by creating a community of photographers nationwide who provide free portrait sessions; (2) the Baby Box Project, which provides a box of infant care necessities to low-income families; (3) Sea Smarts, which offers a series of ocean health education and hands-on, art-based learning opportunities that culminate in community beach clean-ups; (4) Art Heals, which provides art kits through which victims of domestic violence can create art to express themselves; and (5) Give a Girl a Lab Coat, which addresses the K-12 gender gap in science and technology fields by creating a two-week STEM summer camp for middle school girls. The ANNpower Vital Voices initiative gives grants to up to 50 such projects per year.

I had the chance to attend the ANNpower Vital Voices Forum in New York City in June 2016. Here are some excerpts from a blog I wrote about one day of the Forum:

We run like Olympic sprinters from the plush black buses into the Ann Taylor store in Rockefeller Center, still abuzz after the previous evening's invigorating night of shopping and pizza. Our feet, 100 strong, descend the stairs and we are greeted by the sight of an elaborate breakfast. The energy of the room increases ten-fold as we notice the gift bags located under our seats. Then, the panelists arrive and the day begins in earnest.

This second full day of the ANNpower Vital Voices Leadership Forum has been beyond extraordinary. The morning commenced with a panel of inspiring women with impressive media backgrounds. Although they all shared interesting and compelling stories, I was particularly intrigued by Casey Lewis, the co-founder of the CloverLetter, an online journalism platform and newsletter for girls. I've been a loyal reader of Clover since its debut and dreamed of writing for them. As an aspiring journalist, it was a thrill to meet and speak with an innovator and entrepreneur in the journalism space. Casey and the other panelists reminded us to trust ourselves and our abilities, but to be open to feedback and advice as we continue on our journeys.

The morning became even more exciting when we returned to the Summit Room at the Ann Inc. offices and had the opportunity to participate in incredible discussions with Kay Krill, the former CEO of Ann Inc., and Anne Fulenwider, the Editor-in-Chief of Marie Claire magazine. Although Kay's success as a female executive proved highly motivational, given Anne's journalistic focus and rise from editor of her high school paper to editor of a top fashion magazine, I was thrilled to hear from her. She reminded us to shed our doubts because they will only hold us back, and encouraged us to take risks and pursue new endeavors. She said that opportunities arise at unpredictable times and you have to be ready to take bold leaps to benefit from them. This was a consistent theme from speakers throughout the day. They encouraged us to push the limits of our comfort zones and embrace failure. As a perfectionist, typically fearful about any form of failure, this advice encouraged me to reconsider some of my own priorities and challenge my preconceptions of success.

We also heard from Reshma Saujani, the founder of

"Girls Who Code," an organization that aims to close the gender gap in technology and engineering by teaching girls to code. Given her background in law and politics, Reshma is living proof that someone can excel in both the humanities and STEM. Her story transformed and empowered me. I've all-but-abandoned my attitude that I can't conquer math and I'm now open to possibilities in the world of STEM. Her motto resonated with me, "Embrace not being excellent."

In the afternoon, we had a second work session with Kathleen Friery, this time focusing on honing our projects [more on this below] into a 30-second elevator pitch. She reminded us to be concise and provoke emotion. I later had the opportunity to give her my pitch and receive feedback on my idea. Given her background in television and media training and the journalistic focus of my project, I felt incredibly grateful to be able to get the advice and counsel of someone who truly understands and believes in my project. She helped me think of ways to explain my concept more clearly, use emotion more effectively, connect my work to the work of the other girls at the conference, and take my proposal to new heights.

Overall, the day emboldened me and galvanized my commitment to pursue and grow my idea. The experiences and advice of the mentors demonstrated to me that I need to follow my heart, focusing on activities that give me joy. Motivated by the female journalists and executives, it's clear to me that I want my project to be centered around journalism – that's the force that has shaped my life and I want to use it to help those around me.

After another exciting evening that included attending a Broadway play, we returned to the hotel we now call "home." Though tired after a long day, we chattered happily, our conversations reflecting the energy that emanates from the streets of New York. Our glee after a day of revelations and fun tinged with a note of sadness as we realize the Forum ends tomorrow morning. Still, we all know that the doors opened over the last few days will change our lives forever. Thank you ANNpower!

This story is powerful at many levels and demonstrates some of the advantages given to Gen Z as it pursues its commitment to improving the social good. First, a major corporation and a group of adult women, realizing the potential of Gen Z girls, has invested in bringing together 50 of them each summer to hone their leadership skills, raise their consciousness, and encourage social entrepreneurship. Second, they help the girls ideate around concepts that will have real community impact. Third, they challenge the girls to form their ideas into grant-worthy projects and fund them up to $2500 each. The partial list of projects above indicates the success of the program – Gen Z girls are changing the world for the better, one community at a time, fueled by the ANNpower program and their own ingenuity and hard work.

My own ANNpower project gives a sense of how one member of Gen Z is able to mix entrepreneurial instincts with a concern for the community . . . and benefit from the largesse of a major corporation at the same time. When I learned that many members of my generation (especially girls) were being rendered voiceless by cutbacks in many high school journalism programs and school papers, I created a model for a summer journalism seminar, aiming to give girls passionate about journalism the skills and platform they needed to express themselves. Although there are many programs training young people in STEM, languages, and sports, journalism has no similar programs, perhaps because many consider it a dying profession.

Armed with a local grant and sponsorships that covered 100% of the costs, the pilot program exposed 12 girls to a range of journalistic forms via guest speakers, experiential learning activities, tours of journalistic workplaces, and daily assignments. The girls were of multiple races and ethnicities and hailed from eight different schools, which brought varied and interesting perspectives to the seminar. Creating the seminar content and leading the girls was challenging. I wondered if I had the experience and skill to teach them anything. I was concerned they might be bored.

Not surprisingly, the seminar wasn't perfect. Speakers were late and transportation fell through. Some activities exceeded the time allotted, others were too short. While everyone, including me, seemed tentative and timid to start, by the end students were out on the street conducting interviews, asking probing questions of guest speakers, and creating thoughtful pieces via a variety of different mediums.

I, too, felt fulfilled. I had learned to be OK taking on the role of "adult, teacher, and mentor." After the program ended, I connected with each girl individually, giving them a carefully curated list of follow-up activities and mentors. Bolstered by the experience, I applied for and received a

$2500 grant from ANNpower to morph the summer program into an ongoing, monthly training program, at first in my hometown and, eventually, nationally.

Gen Z Community Consciousness Profile: Nadya Okamoto

Gen Z's commitment to helping improve the world is constantly on display in the form of inspirational teens doing amazing things. One outstanding example of a Gen Z leader making a difference is Nadya Okamoto. Her personal story is compelling and her work is highly impactful. I am lucky to know her. Nadya is an 18-year-old from Portland, Oregon, and is the Founder and Executive Director of Camions of Care. She started her freshman year at Harvard College in September 2016. Camions of Care is a youth-run, global nonprofit that strives to manage and celebrate menstrual hygiene through advocacy, youth leadership, and service, primarily through the global distribution of feminine hygiene products.

What ignited your Gen Z consciousness and commitment to helping others?

In the spring of my freshman year of high school, my mother lost her job, and within weeks we could no longer afford our home. We had no choice but to move out and enter what I call our "time of transition," several months of legal homelessness, couch-surfing with our closest friends, who have since become like family. During this time, my commute to school changed from twelve minutes to over two hours each way, with two bus transfers. While having conversations with women who were in much worse living situations than I was, both on my commutes to school and at the shelter, I had an awakening in acknowledging privilege as a spectrum.

How did this realization about your place on the privilege spectrum lead to your first understanding the need that homeless women had for feminine hygiene products?

I found my purpose in trying to figure out how to address a great need I discovered through those talks: menstrual hygiene. I recall one conversation specifically, in the fall of my sophomore year of high school, when I was on my way home from mock trial practice and transferring buses in Old Town in Portland. I approached my bus stop, where a woman I regularly saw sat, cozying up for the night. She was friendly, and we had talked regularly when I visited on my way home in the late evenings. I had finally built up the courage to ask her about what she found most challenging. She told me periods "absolutely sucked" and made her feel "dirty" and "poor." I responded by handing her an extra pad from my bag and she began to cry happy tears. She said she was so surprised that someone had felt comfortable to talk to her about periods, and listen to her needs and respond.

What spurred you into action on the issue?

In March of my Sophomore year of high school, I found myself in an abusive relationship, and right after my family had gained our apartment back, I found myself sitting on a couch at a battered women's shelter in downtown Portland. My knees were hugged tightly to my chest, my forehead throbbed, my lips felt chapped, and the left side of my face felt puffy and painful from where I had been hit. My heart was beating fast from the anxiety and fear that coursed through my body. At the age of 16, I had checked myself into a shelter because I wanted to hide my bruises from my mother, who I had witnessed sacrificing so much and working so hard to bring our family out of legal homelessness and back into our own apartment. At that point in my life, I was consistently keeping a journal. Almost every night before going to sleep, I would write in my journal about my day and record the stories of many of the homeless women I met. During the weekend I spent at the shelter by myself, I realized in looking back at my journal, that I noted menstrual hygiene as a need shockingly often. I had collected an anthology of stories of women using toilet paper, stollen pillowcases, and most commonly brown paper grocery bags, to maintain their periods. I wrote down quotes from the women of how scared they were to ask for menstrual hygiene products because they were embarrassed about their periods, but also how poor menstrual hygiene caused them so much discomfort. I noted how nervous they seemed to chat with me about their periods as if it was a forbidden topic.

How did you turn your awareness about the issue into the inspiration that prompted you to found Camions of Care?

After my weekend at the battered women's shelter, I realized how fortunate I was to have access to educational opportunities and still have confidence in my potential, and I knew I had to do something to act upon this unaddressed natural need of menstrual hygiene for the women I had met. I talked to shelters and nonprofits and found that none of them provided menstrual hygiene products continuously, either due to a lack of resources or a lack of displayed need. Thus, there was this never-ending cycle of organizations not prioritizing menstrual hygiene and women in need being too afraid to advocate for it — leaving periods completely unaddressed. After my family regained stability, I knew I had to do something to make menstrual hygiene more accessible for all women and girls, no matter their circumstances.

So, I founded Camions of Care.

This is more than a domestic issue among homeless women, there's an international dimension as well, isn't there?

On a global level, I learned that periods are the number one reason why girls miss school in developing countries. I also learned that a girl's first period (menarche), in signifying the official transition from girlhood into womanhood, was the single most common event leading to a girl dropping out of school, getting married at a very young age, being socially isolated, or worse, undergoing female genital mutilation. I learned that in Kenya, girls miss an average of 4.9 days of school each month because of a lack of access to adequate menstrual hygiene. In rural Uganda, girls miss up to the 8 days of school each term. That is almost a full week of class — 25 percent of one school month. Think about that…because of periods, girls are missing almost a whole quarter of their classes. In India, 70 percent of reproductive diseases are caused by poor menstrual hygiene, and the effects can go so far as to affect maternal mortality. When it comes to global development, in working to advance families and break the cycle of poverty, women's empowerment is the key—and a major obstacle that stands in the way of bringing all women to the forefront is the taboo surrounding the topic of menstruation.

How is Camions of Care organized and what are some of your achievements so far?

Camions of Care is now a youth-run global nonprofit that celebrates menstrual hygiene through advocacy, youth leadership, and service. We do this through two major programs at the moment: (1) the global distribution of menstrual hygiene products; and (2) the engagement of youth leadership through a nationwide network of campus chapters. Youth leadership is a component that is an integral part of identity. As an organization, we acknowledge the powerful potential held by youth as the leaders of our future. In the last two years we have addressed over 25,000 periods through over 40 nonprofit partners in 17 states and 9 countries. We continue to expand our chapter network from 34 established at universities and high schools around the United States. My business partner and one of my best friends, Vincent Forand, maximized the extensive impact of our organization so that for every dollar that is donated to our organization, we are able to provide another woman or girl in need with everything she needs for an entire menstrual cycle. Every contribution makes a significant difference and goes directly to serving women and girls in need. We are constantly hoping to grow our network of advocates for our menstrual movement, and always welcome helping hands, eager supporters, or inspired youth leaders wanting to take initiative with our cause themselves. We hope everyone will join us in our fight to de-stigmatize menstrual hygiene and our journey to make menstrual hygiene more accessible for women and girls no matter their circumstances.

What other initiatives are you currently working on?

Running Camions of Care has fueled the fire within me to enact systemic social change, especially around women's health. This fall, I started my freshman year at Harvard, where I plan to study political science and public health. I will also be a Thinx Brand Ambassador on the Harvard campus. I am proud of the work we've been able to do, and excited to keep growing Camions of Care into a sustainable menstrual equity organization while growing personally into an impactful women's health advocate.

How can others help?

You can get involved with Camions of Care by starting a chapter with other youth from your area and start a menstruation station at your school to make feminine hygiene products more accessible! Collect items with a feminine hygiene product drive. Contribute to our cause. Spread word about our organization by sharing our videos. Every amount of support makes a difference and we hope you join our #menstrualmovement.

Chapter 6
Gen Z: Non-Partisan but Pro-World

AARON BROWN moves busily around the offices of the Oregon Bus Project, filing papers, sending emails, and giving orders to dutiful volunteers. He holds a cup of coffee in one hand, a handful of pens in the other, and has a phone wedged between his head and shoulder. His expression is a mixture of panic and giddy anticipation as he orders around volunteers and staff members alike. "Hey how's the pizza order coming?" he asks a high school intern. "Oh, hello, Congresswoman," he says into his iPhone, turning away from those who might overhear him. The Bus Project office crackles with energy, as Brown organizes his latest venture, National Voter Registration Day.

The Bus Project is an organization that is in the right place at the right time. Though the Bus Project is run by Millennials, its avowed target is Gen Z. They are trying to crack the code on how to encourage civic engagement among America's next group of voters. Gen Z is fully ready to play its part in improving America and the world as the previous chapter on community consciousness indicates. However, the key to understanding Gen Z engagement is that we focus on issues not politics, results and outcomes not partisan victories. I like to say that Gen Z is non-partisan but pro-world.

The National Voter Registration Day project demonstrated the power of Gen Z's commitment to civic engagement. The city-wide effort was organized by students and was aimed at students – any student who was 17 and older was eligible to register. The enthusiasm generated on a school-by-school basis was impressive and the sign-ups exceeded the Bus Project's projections. An effort was made to register people living in close proximity to the school, including in some economically-challenged neighborhoods. It was incredibly gratifying to register some senior citizens to vote who had never before cast a ballot.

Voting shouldn't be a partisan issue and it's one that does resonate among Gen Z. Voting is one of the most basic expressions of individual "voice" and, as such, is a basic human right. Regrettably, National Voter Registration Day inevitably brings into focus concerns about access to voting. An issue that many thought had been settled in America, voting rights became controversial again with the Supreme Court's 2013 decision in the *Shelby County v. Holder* case. Writing for the majority in the Supreme Court's 5-4 decision, Chief Justice John Roberts asserted, "Our country has changed, and while any racial discrimination in voting is too much, Congress must ensure that the legislation it passes to remedy that problem speaks to current conditions." While seemingly neutral in its impact, the Supreme Court decision undermined the protections inherent in the "Voting Rights Act of 1965" and has caused major issues in certain Southern and Midwestern states, where legislatures systematically have impeded access to voting by the elderly, members of minority communities, and students, all in the name of combatting voter "fraud."

As National Voter Registration Day came to an end, Brown discussed the reality of the struggle for voting rights as a crowd of over 50 volunteers, activists, and elected officials gathered for an intimate after party celebration at a rustic warehouse in Portland's Lloyd district. Many in the crowd were from Gen Z. "It is the chief responsibility of organizations like The Bus Project Foundation to make voting more accessible, more engaging, and more relevant to a broader swath of the American public. We choose to focus on working on voter registration with young populations, and the work that we do is all about making the process of voting something that is more accessible and easier to participate in," Brown says excitedly. "The Bus Project was really excited to participate in National Voter Registration Day and register over 1000 people to vote in one day, because of voting's importance in making democracy more relevant and building power, so that younger folks can hold their politicians accountable to issues young people care about in overwhelming numbers, including climate change, including LGBTQ rights, including police brutality, including college debt and student debt." Brown's brief remarks are met by applause and cheers as the band begins to play in the background.

As Scott Hess of Spark has observed, Gen Z's defaults are toward diversity, environmentalism, globalism, equal rights, and freedom — what were thought of as "progressive" causes to earlier generations but are the status quo for Gen Z. I call those issues "non-partisan" because they should be. How can the 76% of Gen Z who are very concerned about mankind's impact on the planet be considered "partisan?" Gen Z accepts global warming as real and looks for ways to take action, both as individuals and as motivators of collective action. That's the pro-world part.

Gen Z thinks globally because we are so interconnected, with 60 percent wanting to "change the world" (compared with 39 percent of Millennials). We find inspiration in the stories of our peers from around the world. For example, one Gen Z hero is one of our own, Malala Yousafzai, from Pakistan. Yousafzai is the first member of our generation to win the Nobel Peace Prize. Her book, *I Am Malala*, tells of her incredible journey from Taliban victim to international celebrity, all because she wanted to exercise her right to attend school. Her near death experience after being shot by the Taliban inspired her to become an advocate for global access to education – another issue that is fundamentally non-partisan. Malala's book and the movie made from the book show a girl who is like lots of other Gen Z girls from around the world – she has homework, doesn't always get perfect grades, fights with her siblings, and plays video games. Her "normality" helps Gen Z see her extraordinary courage and passion to change the world as achievable.

Speaking of Gen Z leaders, say hello to Gabe Fleisher, an eighth grader from University City, Missouri. Gabe has a passion for politics and history, as well as for informing and engaging people in the news. He is the driving force behind *Wake Up to Politics*, a daily political newsletter (www.wakeuptopolitics.com). The newsletter's mission is to provide a look at the day's news that matters and a quasi-insider view of what governmental movers and shakers are up to. A typical day's issue covers the President, Congress, the courts, elections, and history, and just to keep you on your toes, Gabe throws in a daily trivia question.

Incredibly, Gabe has been putting out *Wake Up to Politics* since he was nine. His goal has remained the same – "to inform readers with the most non-partisan and comprehensive yet understandable version of the news that really matters." You could call that the modern version of the *New York Times*' "All the News That's Fit to Print." I see Gabe as on the cutting edge of Gen Z involvement in the world. The word that jumps out at me in his self-description is the same one I've used above, "non-partisan." While that's a word that is increasingly lost in "adult" political discourse, it's one that typifies Gen Z engagement in the world.

Gabe's story is instructive. He fell in love with politics and history after attending the 2009 presidential inauguration. A couple of years later, he began publishing his own daily political email blast, which he called *The Daily Rundown.* His only subscriber was his mother. *Wake Up to Politics* is sent to about 1200 readers a day. It's content is 100% created by Gabe, who publishes the newsletter before heading to school each morning. A proud Gen Z tech native, Gabe also runs the *Wake Up to Politics* Twitter and Facebook accounts, which are followed by over 3500 people. He has interviewed political and legal figures such as Debbie Wasserman Schultz and Sandra Day O'Connor, covered presidential debates, attended primary caucus meetings, and written a book, a history of his elementary school. He has attracted the attention of NPR's "Talk of the Nation," appeared on MSNBC's "Up with Steve Kornacki," and been covered by *Politico*, the *Washington Post*, *Salon*, and the *St. Louis Post-Dispatch*.

Gabe is emblematic of many of the themes we've seen throughout this book. Enabled by technology, he has shown a relentless entrepreneurial spirit as he has pursued and developed a personal interest. His approach is decidedly non-partisan but pro-world – he wants to engage readers of all ages with interesting and informative content about politics in a America, hoping that a more informed public will be a more engaged public. A recent *Wake Up to Politics* newsletter highlighted the fact that it was a certain number of days until a Presidential Debate, a certain number of days until Election Day 2016, and a certain number of days until Gabe's 15th birthday.

Gen Z is already making a difference on the world scene. In the 1940s, a girl sitting in the United States wouldn't have known about the specifics of the horrors unfolding in Europe in the form of the Nazi holocaust and couldn't have played a role in bringing the issues to light. Today, Gen Z sees images of the Anne Franks of today stuck in Aleppo at grave risk of extermination by the next Syrian government or Russian bombing raid. With social media at their disposal, Gen Z can speak out to urge a humanitarian solution, whether it be to advocate for the United States to take in more Syrian refugees or the UN to take meaningful action to stop the carnage.

Gen Z is already showing itself to be different from

previous generations. Drug use, alcohol consumption (38 percent drop), smoking, and teen pregnancy (40 percent drop) are all at their lowest levels in decades. This is not to say that Gen Z is perfect, only to indicate that my expectation that Gen Z can become the next "Greatest Generation" is realistic and possible.

Non-partisan, pro-world profile: Claire Devine

Claire Devine is a Junior at Jesuit High School in Portland, Oregon. She is devoted to global issues as well as making a change within her community. Claire is the Undersecretary of Oregon Model United Nations as well as a Young Leader with the Oregon World Affairs Council. She also works with the KINO Border Initiative to spread awareness of migration issues and change policies surrounding them. She is passionate about domestic politics as well, working as an intern at the Bus Project.

How have you demonstrated your interest in civic engagement generally and politics in particular?

When I discovered my interest in politics and justice in middle school, I started off by writing controversial papers for almost every essay assignment, hoping to increase discussion surrounding issues in my isolated Christian school community. Once I got to high school, however, I met a group of likeminded students through Model United Nations, and instantly threw myself into the club. I also occasionally worked at the Bus Project with a close friend. As a leader of my school Model UN Club, and eventually the under-secretary for Oregon High School International Relations League Model United Nations, I now strive to create as accurate a simulation of the actual UN as I can with our limited resources. At the upcoming conference for Oregon high schools, I will be pioneering the first International Court of Justice committee in the history of our state conference. Additionally, I have submitted articles on immigration, sex education, and reproductive justice to both national and local newspapers and magazines. On a smaller scale, I will be managing my school's efforts to register voters on National Voter Registration Day.

Are most young people today engaged by politics and the political system or by specific issues?

I think that the majority of teenagers are swayed considerably by the media. In wanting to conform to societal norms, young people grab onto whatever political identity — good or bad — is slapped onto them. However, I doubt that most teens actually put time into researching their political leanings, thus creating a lack of sincerity and decreasing personal commitment to specific causes. I think that most attachment to politicians remains at the emotional level, and is short-lived. I do believe, however, that when teens are personally affected by policies, their voice in the political scene often proves to be the most influential.

Are the political sentiments of young people the same or different from past generations?

Recently, I have noticed that young people, including myself, are increasingly distancing themselves from actual political institutions, and moving more towards the support of grassroots organizations.

What is your stance on climate change?

The more that I explore my interest in politics and justice, the more important this issue becomes to me. I am a HUGE believer in global climate change, and I sincerely believe that if global warming is not immediately and radically addressed, it will result in our ultimate demise.

On an issue like climate change, why do young people seem to be passionate about the issue while many members of the older generation deny there is an issue or turn a blind eye?

To put it plainly, our generation has an actual stake in the future of our planet. The older generation can continue destroying natural resources while not having to suffer any of the grave consequences in their lifetime. In contrast, with the direction that our environment is headed, the younger generation has every reason to fear diminishing natural resources, mass extinctions, global floods, etc., occurring during our lifetimes and our children's lifetimes.

Why is it important that young people help take action to prevent climate change? What are you currently doing?

Like I said before, our generation is directly impacted by the steps we take to reverse global climate change. This year, I am taking an environmental science course at my school in order to further understand the root causes of climate change, and plan out concrete actions to reverse this trend. I am also an active member of our Green Team.

What goals and ambitions do you have for the future?

In the future, I hope to study International Relations and Philosophy so that I can someday work for the United Nations or a global NGO, working on either human rights issues or the environment. Other than my own goals, I hope to someday see the international cooperation of all countries, and the voices of the marginalized promoted on the global stage.

Chapter 7

Gen Z: Experiential Activities Are Key

NICARAGUA. It is a country of dust, at least in the non-rainy season. The dust is everywhere — on your shoes, clothes, sticking to your skin, blowing into your eyes. Every car that goes by creates a mini dust storm, as the tires kick a cloud of dust in your direction. Amazingly, after centuries of exploitation by foreign powers and domestic leaders, and in spite of the Nicaragua's status as the second poorest country in our hemisphere (only Haiti is poorer), the people are happy, warm, and welcoming.

For the past three years, I have journeyed to rural villages in Nicaragua. For someone raised in middle class comfort in the United States, the scenes of quotidian life in Nicaragua are shocking. One village where I worked, El Trohilo, consists of corrugated metal houses with no electricity or running water stuck in the middle of sugar cane fields. Flies cover emaciated cattle and horses. Children kick ball-shaped trash in a street game of soccer. Plastic bags and discarded packaging blow across the disheartening bleak landscape.

Like many of my fellow members of Gen Z, I have valued

the opportunity to experience the world. In fact, some have called Gen Z the "experiential generation" because of our embrace of trying and doing things, and picking ourselves up and moving on if things don't work out. Some 77% of us are extremely or very interested in volunteering to gain work experience and, according to a DeepFocus study, 89% of us say that we prefer to spend our free time in activities that we consider productive and creative instead of just "hanging out."

I'm not alone in seeking international experiences. Kristen Kelley, the CMO of Randstad, points out that Gen Z can experience other countries via Skype, Periscope, and Snapchat, which spurs a high appetite for international opportunities. Studies show that Gen Z is far less possessions-oriented than Millennials, putting far greater emphasis on "shareworthy" experiences. These can run the gamut from a walk in the park with friends to the kind of deep immersion in a foreign culture that I have experienced.

Last year, I led a 14-person trip to a different village, San Juan de La Concepcion. I stayed with a family in what they considered to be "guest" quarters. Separated from the main family house, my room consisted of cinder block walls, a dirt floor, and a lumpy mattress of ancient origins. There was no electricity, which meant a relatively early bedtime given the lack of lights. That was a good thing because the roosters started crowing around 4:00 am.

Naturally, I've learned far more from the Nicaraguan girls I'm supposed to be helping as a Girl Rising ambassador than they've learned from me. Yes, I have excited them by showing them my iPad or allowing them to take pictures with my iPhone – they were entranced by the capabilities of these devices and delighted by seeing their selfies. One of the best things we did in El Trohilo was print out a picture of each child in the school where I worked and place them into frames that we had helped the kids make. I felt confident that other than some religious symbols that these photos would be the primary decorative element in their houses.

One of the benefits of Gen Z's optimistic outlook on life is that life becomes an adventure – and that we have the confidence to explore and experience new areas. For example, last February, I worked with a classmate to organize a community discussion about the highly-charged issue of police use of force, an issue that continues to dominate the news cycle and wreak havoc in communities across the country. I remember the event vividly and also wrote an essay about it:

"What you need to do is stop killing our sons," screamed the African-American woman as she looked menacingly into the eyes of the white female police detective. Her indignant comments tinged with sorrow hung heavily in the air. The room fell silent. Nervous eyes darted back and forth between the two women. Things were falling apart. I had to act…but didn't know what to do.

Two months earlier, sitting in "Crime and Punishment," a course examining the state of the U.S. justice system, I had pondered our task – a final project probing the issue of police use of force. Chatting with my classmate, Jessica, I discovered our mutual exasperation about the spate of police shootings of unarmed men and women in Portland, events that had thrown the city into turmoil. We agreed that the polarizing nature of the issue had thwarted the city's meager attempts to foster understanding and compromise.

Perhaps naively, we decided to organize a community forum concerning police use of force. It would feature individuals from divergent sides of the debate with the aim of spurring positive, meaningful dialogue and establishing common ground. Dave, our teacher, was dubious but supported our efforts. While neither Jessica nor I had experienced police violence, the issue quickly became our own as we encountered the raw emotions of those we invited to participate. We found a location for the event, set a date, and finalized the speakers.

As we planned, Jessica and I were forced to confront our drastically different perspectives. The daughter of parents who collected Black Panther and Che posters and were proud to call themselves "liberal," I was highly skeptical of police behavior. Jessica, the daughter of a judge and federal prosecutor, grew up surrounded by police officers. Our disagreements and struggles to work together seemed a microcosm of the larger conversation and conciliation we hoped to achieve.

The day arrived. The community center filled with a highly diverse crowd. We had done our job, or so I thought. We introduced the panelists – a police detective, public defender, Black Lives Matter representative, state prosecutor, head of a Black Student Union, college professor. The ground rules were strict, enforcing the idea of dialogue and education, not debate. Each panelist spoke, *articulating disparate views. They disagreed, but avoided hostility, listening intently and respectfully.*

The room's energy shifted dramatically with the "stop killing our sons" outburst, anguished aggression aimed directly at the police detective. We'd invited honest conversation, but this threatened to derail the event. I glanced at my teacher who sat off to the side. He mouthed the words, "Do something!"

Naturally non-confrontational, I wanted to hide or slink away. Instead, I steeled myself, realizing it was a moment to demonstrate courage. "Thank you," I said, interrupting the woman's diatribe. "I recognize your anger and pain." I took a halting breath, "But the point of this event is to listen and learn, even when you disagree." She tried to continue speaking, but I cut her off with an insistent but plaintive, "Please."

The woman clenched her fists and started to rise from her seat. Then, she nodded, sitting again, saying, "I get it. Sorry." The discussion progressed, a positive feeling building in fits and starts. No one could deny the empathy of the police detective. Everyone felt the pain of the woman who had lost her son. Answers seemed less theoretical and more possible.

Healing the wounds surrounding the issue of police use of force will take time. We won't bridge the divides in a single meeting, but our forum was a start. Since the event, I've organized a series of articles on police issues for a teen website and we are working with a local attorney to stage a series of similar discussions on a larger scale in Portland. The issue is complex, the solution uncertain.

But, I will continue to do my part to advance the conversation.

My experience in organizing the police forum was instructive. First, when Jessica and I set out to create the forum, we had no idea that it would be the first such gathering in Portland – it took two naïve girls from Gen Z to come up with such a simple idea for dialogue. Second, although we had no idea how to organize such an event, there was ample opportunity to learn on the job – we went to experts, asked questions, inquired about best practices, followed sound models. Our greatest asset was our willingness to try, a core Gen Z attribute.

Perhaps the most meaningful experience I've had over the last couple of years came in the form of an after school program I co-created for six and seven-year-olds from an inner city charter school. Our experience came in the form of giving them an experience different from their typical classroom activities. Although neither my co-creator nor I had ever taught that age group (or, perhaps *because* we had never worked with that age group), we decided to challenge them with big, complex problems.

So, the first week we were with them, we focused the activities and discussions around race. The group is highly diverse, but like most kids that age they are generally oblivious to race, at least superficially. We discovered that notwithstanding their age and generally sunny outlook on life, they had already picked up subtle, but real inklings of prejudice. We hoped that sensitizing them to those inappropriate stereotypes or modes of thought at a young age might inoculate them against actions based on prejudice in the future.

As the weeks proceeded, we tackled similarly challenging topics, everything from gender to gentrification to inequality. I was amazed by the awareness and insights of kids so young – the lower end of the Gen Z generational spectrum. As with my experience in Nicaragua, there was just as much learning on my side as on the side of the kids.

Experiential Profile: Zhang Chenyu

Zhang Chenyu is a teenager from Yunnan, China, a province in southwestern China bordering Myanmar, Laos, and Vietnam with a varied landscape encompassing snow-capped mountains, rice terraces, lakes, and deep gorges. Yunnan is home to 26 of China's 55 minority ethnic groups, including the Yi, Bai, and Di people. Chenyu belongs to the Yi minority and is not Han Chinese (as are 90% of all people in Mainland China). His status as a member of a Chinese minority group has driven many of his experiential and service activities.

What kinds of experiential activities have engaged you.

The projects and initiatives I undertake are mainly related to the geography, history, and condition of resources of the Yunnan region. I focus a lot on my ethnic group, which has witnessed a lot of migration of people from the mountains, where the Yi people originated, to more urban locations. The Yi People and people from other ethnic groups move to cities in order to find jobs with better pay. The work conditions in the cities can be quite harsh, so I have set up workplace safety seminars. I have also frequently visited my ancestral hometown, where there are a number of WWII veterans. I have conducted interviews with them as part of an oral history project.

Give us the international perspective on Gen Z's interest in experiential activities.

Achieving something meaningful in life is the collective result of resources, willpower, and passion. Recent history has seen more and more opportunity for interesting experiences for people of different backgrounds, especially in more developed countries. Now, youngsters with ideas can gain support with resources such as Kickstarter and other online platforms. These opportunities allow many from our generation to achieve things more efficiently and with fewer obstacles than our parents and grandparents.

Is it important to have meaning behind the experiential things you do and those around you do?

Yes it is. Different people perceive different meanings behind their tasks. The more meaningful a task becomes to us, the more passion we will have to perform a job with well-rounded consideration. It's very important to have meaning behind what I do. For example, in my town we have a lot of high school student initiatives, including a non-profit that helps a local primary school headed by a girl I know. She does a fantastic job because she really cares about what she does. She told me that the first time she went to the primary school she was in awe of how smart the kids were but how limited they were by their lack of resources. This reality has really motivated her.

Are there areas where you continue to struggle to find meaning?

I truly value spending time with family. However, the day before yesterday was Chinese mid-autumn festival. It is a day for families to come together to have a special dinner together. My extended family came to my house to celebrate. That said, I missed almost all of the celebration in order to attend an online class. Although I crave academic success, I was crushed to not be able to spend time with my family. In the process of finding meaning I want to continue to try to think about why I am doing what I am doing and why it matters.

What do you think needs to happen to encourage more young people to find meaning in their experiential activities?

Before I saw the migrant workers in my village, I had never really acknowledged their plight or understood that I could help them. Yet, via the experiences I have had I built an emotional connection with the workers I saw in my village and gained the confidence to make a difference in their lives. I think that young people need to experience first hand the importance of finding meaning in their daily life in order to work towards changing the culture that we live in. The more teenagers who expose themselves to the world, the better chance that they will find meaning in their lives. That said, I acknowledge that this change will happen slowly.

What goals do you have for the future?

When I was nine or 10 years old, I visited my ancestral village. There are many international NGOs that support my village – the International Red Cross, Turner International, etc. However, most volunteers stay only for a couple of weeks and then leave. However, I got to meet an American doctor who came to our village and set up a local hospital. He brought his family. He lived in the village. At first, we treated him like an outsider, but soon he became part of our community. This doctor ended up staying for two years in the village — he didn't want to leave but his job sent him somewhere else. When he left, the entire village went to see him off. That was when I said to myself, "When I grow up, I want to be someone like that." I don't know what my future will look like exactly, but I still have that ambition.

Chapter 8
Gen Z: The First Post-Race, Post-Gender Generation

A RECENT ARTICLE on the front page of the *New York Times Thursday Styles* section introduced many adults to a Gen Z trendsetter, Rowan Blanchard. The 14-year-old star of the Disney Channel show "Girl Meets World," Blanchard is the archetypal Gen Z kid and breaks the mold of previous Disney girl stars such as Demi Lovato, Miley Cyrus, and Selena Gomez. Blanchard, who has 4.5 million followers on Instagram and 500,000 followers on Twitter, recently made a six-minute film for writer/director Carrie Brownstein and identifies as "queer," "not because she necessarily is gay or bisexual, but because she isn't necessarily not." While Blanchard's leads a bi-coastal lifestyle as she shoots her show, attends New York fashion week events, screens her movie, and attends concerts, her Instagram account bio is probably similar to many girls her age: "Lover of Harry Potter, chocolate and Beyonce."

One of the classic messages in U.S. history classes, whether in elementary, middle school, or high school, is that the United States has had a "difficult" past when it comes to discrimination based on race and sexual identity. You learn about slavery, the Civil War, segregation, violence, racism, and the achingly gradual change over the last two hundred years. Throughout these lessons, there is a sense of resignation conveyed that given this history we have to accept that this is just the way things are, that there is no hope for meaningful change, that majority groups will continue to build themselves up by climbing on the backs of minority groups. That said, I'm confident that Gen Z, having grown up at a time when social norms have changed dramatically, will be the first post-race, post-gender generation. Kyle Andrew, CMO of American Eagle Outfitters, did some in-depth research on pre-teens and teens and concluded that Gen Z seems, "to be a lot nicer than other generations: They are not judgmental, they don't put people in boxes, and they don't seem to care as much about what you do, who you love, or what you look like."

Let's look at race. We are all aware of our race and our heritage. I will never forget the activity we did in my first grade class where we had to pair the color of our skin with a spice. I immediately grabbed cinnamon because I loved cinnamon toast, only to be redirected by the teacher that "onion powder" might be more appropriate. Yet, although Gen Z is "aware" of race and background, race is not something that defines how we perceive others or how we interact with them. Ours is the last generation in which whites will be in the majority in the United States (comprised of 47 percent ethnic minorities, Gen Z is the most ethnically diverse generation in U.S. history), and we have grown up in a world in which the barriers and divides between races are becoming increasingly mixed and blurred.

When we meet people, we do not immediately judge or classify them based on race. Instead, we bond over similarities in personality, celebrate their accomplishments, appreciate their success, compassion, or humor. Although we certainly "see" race, we have grown up in a world where anyone and everyone can be our friend. We create connections first and think about racial and cultural differences second, celebrating and emphasizing the importance of our difference, but not allowing it to become divisive or to drive separation.

We are not color blind, but we are more color accepting. Unlike our parents, we have never existed in a world where segregation and racial violence were the norm. It is important to acknowledge that this transformation is not complete — for members of Gen Z on the older end of the age spectrum, some issues are still evident. However, by the time our younger brothers and sisters are of age, things will look radically different.

Let's look at gender. Twenty years ago, a woman running for president would have seemed impossible. Yet, for members of Gen Z it seems like the norm. The first presidential primary election that many of us remember was in 2008, when Hillary Clinton, a woman, took on Barak Obama, an African-American man. For us, it has seemed that anything is possible. We have grown up in a post-Title IX world where women can go to any college they like and where women are no longer expected to stay at home and raise a family if they have different ambitions. As women, we are told from a young age that we can accomplish just as much as our dads and brothers and we do, accomplishing just as much if not more as our male counterparts.

Social inequalities do remain. For women in developing countries and religiously conservative societies, there is much progress still to be made. Even women in the Western world face sexual harassment, unfair wages, and ongoing stereotypes. Still, while the society we exist in may continue to impose these hardships, there has been a fundamental shift in the way we think. Women are now raised to know that our potential is not any less than that of men. As such, even when faced with inequality, we continue to fight to gain the opportunities we know we deserve.

Finally, sexuality. Gen Z has emerged in a world increasingly tolerant of differences in sexual orientation. We understand that a two-sided binary is unrealistic, and a JWT Intelligence survey found that 81 percent of Gen Z "agreed that gender doesn't define a person as much as it used to." We cringe when an online form only gives us two options for gender — male or female — because we know there are so many more. We preface introductions with our preferred gender pronouns. We celebrate the legalization of gay marriage. A study by Northeastern University indicates that 73 percent of Gen Z agreed that everyone should have the right to marry regardless of sexual orientation. We have grown up amongst people who define themselves as gay, transgender, or bisexual. These people are our peers, friends, and relatives. Our favorite TV shows feature characters who openly question their gender and sexuality — think *Orange is the New Black* and *Transparent*. An increasing number of schools host gender neutral bathrooms and encourage gay/straight alliances. We are allowed to be multiple genders or no genders. Love, clothing, and friendship are all flexible. Gen Z is on the forefront of a new world where we are defining for ourselves the values and guidelines that govern our lives. The process is not always easy, but the progress is real.

We take our embrace of the different to our daily lives, especially in our education. My current English class, "Hybrid Identities," is a prime example. In this class, our small but mighty group of 18 students is presented with contemporary literature from a range of authors with diverse perspectives and points of view — from women to members of the LGBTQ community to racially diverse authors. We are encouraged to question what it means to belong and how we can understand ourselves in relation to those who differ from us.

We have been moved by Ta-Nehesi Coates' visceral presentation of the black experience in American society and puzzled through the poetic mixture of Spanish and English in Gloria Anzaldua's description of her experience as an outsider. We've considered the concept that "not all suffering is created equal," presented in JD Vance's "Hillbilly Elegy," and analyzed the memoirs of Sherman Alexis' experience of transitioning from life on an Native American reservation to a white, middle class community. We've looked at what the work of Amy Tan says about the divide between first and second generation immigrants.

It's a typical class as we sit around the table in the seminar-style room and begin our conversation for the day. We are discussing a piece written by Audre Lord, a black, lesbian, socialist. The piece, entitled "Sister Outsider," offers a reflection on the modern feminist movement. Today, two students, Oscar and Helen will lead the class. We start by defining key vocabulary from the text in small groups. My group wrestles with the word "intersectionality." It seems that the word itself is an intersection — one person in my group thinks it has to do with race, another gender, another age. We ultimately decide it is a compilation of many factors, including those we identified. As we come back together in the large group, a student in the class highlights a point made consistently in the reading, that the experience of a white feminist and the oppression she faces is very different from that of a black feminist, who must deal with additional issues due to her race. An African-American student testifies with raw honesty and true vulnerability about the increased dangers faced by blacks in the U.S., an allusion made frequently in the text. I am quick to agree, but note that although the oppression of the white feminist may be less severe, her oppression is not invalidated, it's still real.

Although the conversation initially moved forward awkwardly, it slowly gathers steam as we all begin to feel slightly more comfortable sharing our ideas and perspectives. In many cases the worlds of academic analysis and personal sharing come together. We often don't agree. Yet, we feel protected by the list of "community norms" we developed as a class — "speak from the I perspective," "assume positive intentions," "do not act on judgment."

This class has been a turning point for me. I love the humanities, and have always enjoyed History and English classes. Yet high school classes in these subjects have been dominated by stories about and by white, upper/middle class males. The famous revolutionaries we learned about were all men. Our analysis of U.S. history was always through the eyes of white male property owners and intellectuals. In English class, we read the works of F. Scott Fitzgerald, Mark Twain, and Shakespeare – white men. This literature and these stories painted an image of both women and minorities as illiterate, inept, and subservient.

When teachers did make an effort to include diversity, it was generally nothing more than a lukewarm token. In History, we spent a class period on the women's rights movement. In English, we read a poem by Emily Dickinson. The texts were presented as second class to the works and stories of men, a brief side note in a larger narrative of patriarchy.

I remember two vivid examples. In my U.S. history class junior year, we made it through much of the first semester without hearing a single female voice. When we finally did a reading about women, it was about female sexuality, depicting women as simultaneously cunning and incompetent, completely dependent on men and resorting to selling their bodies to gain a form of "independence." When I asked my teacher when we would read about the feminist movement of the 1950s/1960s, he responded that we were too short on time.

In my American literature class, we read the works of several female voices. Yet, each of the pieces of literature we read painted women as mentally ill and deranged. The poems of Emily Dickinson discussed death and depression, Charlotte Perkins Gillman's "The Yellow Wallpaper" talked of madness and delusions, Sylvia Plaath's poetry foreshadowed her untimely end. I distinctly remember our teacher professing that the female style of the time was one of "drama and emotions," while the male was one of "reason and intellect." Our teacher would prompt us to scrutinize these women, their personal lives and their struggles, de-emphasizing the literary brilliance that remained part of their legacy. We read almost no literature by individuals of color, and for what we did read, the discussions centered almost exclusively on racial discrimination.

This lopsided approach has been the norm in American education for decades, and reflects reality that women and minorities are generally still oppressed in this society. But just because it has become a norm does not make it OK.

I am a white woman from a middle class family, who lives in a city that lacks diversity. My school reflects the city it serves. I would never claim to understand the experiences of someone who is a racial minority or who is economically disadvantaged. But, as someone who also attended five different schools in two different states and one foreign country over the course of just six years, I also have some understanding of what it's like to be considered "other," to be the person who doesn't fit in or whose narrative isn't necessarily consistent with mainstream society's. When I lived in the Netherlands for two years, I felt constantly out of place. I did not speak the language. I did not enjoy the same food or the same sports. I was subjected to glares and reprimands at grocery stores, restaurants, and parks because I was foreign, because I was different. As a result, I developed a complex identity, an identity drawing from numerous cultures, multiple languages, and striking life experiences. All of this in mind, I certainly don't identify with the Anglo-male version of the humanities imposed on me.

I am looking for a change, as are many of my friends from different races, cultures, and backgrounds who have told me they crave the same. This is an imperative, not a mere desire. The face of America is changing. Among Gen Z, complex racial and gender identity is commonplace. In fact, according to Anna Fieler of Popsugar, Gen Z might better be called the "Pluralist Generation" given our easy acceptance of diverse races and religions and a basic belief that "people *can* co-exist in society."

As these societal changes progress, more and more young people don't and can't identify with the white patriarchal narrative that currently dominates the study of the Humanities. This is why classes like my "Hybrid Identities" English class, classes that encourage difficult conversations and that allow us to learn from the works of authors from many different perspectives, are so important. These classes challenge us to analyze disparate voices and allow us to look at the world's rich diversity and complexity as much more than the white, male norm. These classes allow us to both celebrate our ethnic, cultural, racial, and gender-based differences and connect with those identities. We are encouraged to appreciate the fact that we may never fully understand the experiences of people different from us. Yet, we learn that the best way to accept that reality is not by rejecting others, but by trying to find commonality or accepting the fundamental differences.

My experience with this new class is just beginning — there are many more readings and discussions ahead. Honestly, I have no idea what to expect or what will come next. But for now, I am leaning into the discomfort, the uncertainty, the emotions, and celebrating the opportunity to engage with the Humanities in a new, exhilaratingly diverse way.

The progress described above in mind, problems remain, largely due to the fact that we live in a world dominated by older generations accustomed to discrimination based on race, gender, and sexuality. Our parents and older brothers and sisters have grown accustomed to segregation and violence. Unarmed African-American men are shot, women are raped at staggering rates on college campuses, states ban protections for transgender students. As members of Gen Z, we see these persistent problems, we know something is wrong, and we want to do something about it.

Another factor to monitor is the concern that Gen Z over-revs on political correctness. To meet the post-race, post-gender descriptive, Gen Z has to adopt a level of awareness and sensitivity far beyond that of mainstream society – normal Gen Z tolerance and behavior rates as "ultra-PC" to the average American. That said, we can take things too far. I'm all for a vibrant discussion on this topic in order to keep things in perspective. For example:

Should brown rice sushi and yoga be considered "cultural appropriation?"

Is it possible to read Huckleberry Finn in a school context without offending African-Americans and Native Americans?

Should a community center be closed from Friday afternoon through Sunday because of fears that hosting an event during that timeframe might offend people who practice different religions?

We could all offer our own cases of political correctness gone wild. I like what Will Acheampong, a senior at Bellaire High School in Texas, has said on this topic. Will is the founder of a student-driven nonprofit organization called Students Without Borders, an organization that acts as a youth-run parallel to Doctors Without Borders. Talking about political correctness, he has said the following, "I see few benefits of either extreme. I believe that parity can be found between political correctness and other opinions. Forcing others to be politically correct does not change their deep-seated opinions and beliefs. Only meaningful discussion and an open dialogue about contentious and often misunderstood issues can truly begin to change our society for the better — not beating others over the head with the "politically correct stick."

Race, gender, sexuality. These are all words that feed into the larger concept of "intersectionality" discussed briefly above — the concept that each of us is like an intersection, multi-faceted, complex, unable to be pigeonholed and defined by inflexible binaries and a limited array of colors. As a generation, we are collectively working to move society away from a world where race, gender, and sexuality are limiting factors and towards a place where diversity is a celebrated norm. We care. We have seen the potential with the changes that have already manifested themselves, and we will continue to promote change, no matter how long the process takes.

Post-Race, Post-Gender Profile: Tyler White

Tyler White is a junior at De La Salle North Catholic High School in Portland, Oregon. From a young age, he has been engaged with his community on different issues connected to racism and classism. He was born and raised in NE Portland, in the Concordia-Alberta neighborhood, a historically African-American neighborhood which has recently faced the challenge and burden of gentrification. Tyler is a member of his Student Council, the president of his school's Equity and Inclusion Student Union, and the chief blogger and the youth project coordinator for "The I Love This Place PDX" blog and the PLACE Center. Juggling his academic pursuits, social justice advocacy, and athletic activities, Tyler has a well-rounded perspective that has allowed him to be open to the thoughts of others. After college, he hopes to become a high-profile lawyer, humanitarian, politician, and, hopefully, Secretary of State.

What changes have you observed in regards to race, gender, and sexual equality in your lifetime?

The increasing level of acceptance with respect to racial, gender and sexual identities has become a huge movement in recent years. With everything from gender-neutral bathrooms to conversations about racial and gender equality in economic opportunity, there has been an ongoing change, that I am more than happy to be a part of.

What are the critical areas where there is still a lot of work left to do regarding race, gender, and sexual equality?

The major change I have observed is a change in REPRESENTATION and UNDERSTANDING.

Some people say that our generation, Gen Z, is the first "post-race" and "post-gender" generation. Do you agree? Why or why not?

Not necessarily, because I feel that small things happen to break through the stigmas around these issues, but nothing meaningful has begun to happen. Some of the same things that were happening fifty years ago are still prevalent today, especially in regards to race.

What is the role and responsibility of young people to create a more tolerant and accepting world?

In many respects, the responsibility is solely ours. We are the ones who will have to deal with it in the future. So, we need to create and cultivate the society we want, whether that be in our own home or internationally.

What work are you involved with as a young person that relates to this mission?

I have been a part of many events and programs that have been dedicated to providing youth with opportunities to better their surroundings. Additionally, I run a blog about community change and coordinate a youth engagement center.

What potential challenges do you see in coming years? How do you plan to overcome them?

Getting into the college I end up targeting. To get there, I would say I will need to genuinely work as hard as possible, to fulfill and meet the requirements of acceptance, without getting lost in the process and staying true to what it is I believe in or what I wish to accomplish.

Is there any hope for changing the culture and attitudes of the older generations in regards to race, gender, and sexuality? What can/should we as young people do?

No. I feel like changing the attitudes of people our age and younger is my main focus for now. If we achieve that, older generations will naturally follow.

What goals do you have for the future?

Find what success will look like for me. Be happy. Do what it is that I want to do, regardless of the money and accolades. Establish who I am.

Chapter 9
How to Connect to Gen Z

I REALLY ENJOYED a July 2014 article on Shaun McBride, the glib, long-haired Snapchat maven who has built a global following. His followers, known as "Shonduras" made him one of social media's first celebrities and he was rewarded handsomely by youth-oriented brands anxious to tap into his network of Gen Z and Millennial enthusiasts. In his late 20s, McBride is a Millennial, but he exhibited a sensibility and style that connected with a younger demographic as well. Among his sponsors were Taco Bell, Major League Soccer, and Disney, who paid him up to $30,000 each to connect their brand to Snapchat content that attracted Gen Z.

McBride's story is instructive. He was a sales rep for companies in the action sports industry who traveled a lot. He would text photos from his trips back to his six sisters, aged 13 to 22. His siblings told him that communication would be easier via Snapchat, and he began sending them photos with uniquely-styled doodles on top of the photos. Like modern-day PR agents, the sisters shared his photos with friends and his followers grew quickly, eventually allowing him to focus full time on building his community of more than 350,000 "Shonduras" and begin collecting sponsors. He also advises corporate America on connecting to Gen Z via Snapchat.

Snapchat took off as a means of connecting to Gen Z for a variety of reasons. First, as a form of messaging, it was highly individualized. Second, the fact that it disappeared aligned with the mindset and attention span of its user base. Finally, it was the first social media platform that belonged to us – *we* made Snapchat a success, we didn't inherit a popular platform from another generation. That sense of ownership and agency meant a lot.

The story of Snapchat and its connection to and use by Gen Z helps inform this chapter's objective – telling you how to connect to Gen Z, either as a brand or a technology platform. So, what does Gen Z want from brands? The answer is complicated. Gen Z wants lots of things, but it all boils down to three main areas of interest.

First, Gen Z likes simplicity. We want brands that fit seamlessly into our already busy, complex lives. We are very knowledgeable about the products that we consume, but not particularly loyal. If a product or brand isn't working for us, we are likely to make a quick decision to shop around for something better.

This mindset contrasts somewhat with our environmental consciousness and frugality — Deloitte reports that 39 percent of us would rather re-use things we already have instead of buying something new. Growing up during the Great Recession and equipped with an unprecedented ability to vet product purchases, Gen Z is careful about purchases, looking for the best quality at the "right" price. We saw our parents struggle during the recession, making us practical and value conscious, and we are prepared to fight for our future, including employing bargain hunting and financial planning.

A Lincoln Financial survey of 15 to 19-year-olds indicated that 71 percent of Gen Z is focused on saving money for the future (college expenses and post-college choices). Even at a young age, we focus on plans to get a job, finish college, and safeguard money for the future. Here's where the parallel to the previous "Greatest Generation" comes out – that generation, too, was formed by its experience with economic adversity. Gen Z is looking for the best quality at the right price. Interestingly, because we were trained to be savvy shoppers from a young age, we exercise more influence over household purchase decisions than previous generations. An early example of this came a few years ago when Toyota showed a young boy pushing his parents to buy an SUV instead of a minivan so that they would be seen as "hip."

We appreciate brands with a clean, simple, modern atheistic and that project positive, easy vibes in stores and online. According to the Pew Research Center, even though 79 percent of us shop online, 78 percent like shopping in stores, particularly specialty stores that offer affordability, changing styles, and pleasant shopping experiences — names such as Nike, Urban Outfitters, Free People, Vineyard Vines, Nordstrom.

Second, Gen Z wants brands to make it personal. In fact, cmo.com says marketing to us needs to be Personal, Persistent, and Permission-based. We expect companies and brands to engage each of us on a unique level and get us their product in a way that appeals directly to us, and it cannot be traditional television advertising – we've never watched commercials in our entire life. As Mindtree CMO, Paul Gottsegen, says, "Obvious marketing is totally foreign to Gen Z," and suggests that brands should imbed commercials into content.

We yearn to be able to customize and personalize our experiences with products and what we learn about them. For example, we most value recommendations from our friends and we've come to rely on them for product information. The best way to attract us is to collaborate with us, which isn't difficult given how easy it is to communicate with us.

We find our heroes and idols, not the other way around. For example, we idolize YouTube stars like Alexis G. Zall and Teala Dunn, over traditional celebrities because we feel like we can build personal connections with them. While Hollywood movie stars remain elusive in their Beverly Hills mansions, YouTube stars are ordinary people just like us, who respond to our comments and interact with us on social media. We hate "fake," unattainable norms and look for brands that feature, simple, ordinary people.

We follow a broad range of heroes in a way that each of us curates, looking for influencers who can enable us through their connection and promotion of brands. Christine Mi is a Yale undergrad who uses Snapchat to create art that depicts her looking like the objects of iconic paintings and various historical figures. When Ms. Mi connects a brand to her Snapchat art, she endeavors for the brand to be seen as the enabler.

Third, Gen Z craves a sense of independence and voice in connection with the brands we choose to buy. We are a generation of change-makers and we like brands that help us feel as if we are creating our own solutions, brands that make us feel as if we are truly part of the product and its larger mission. And, we want those products to reflect our beliefs and values.

We demand that brands be unique and authentic. A study by Wildness, Inc. found that 94 percent of Gen Z ranked "individualism" as a key characteristic and that "authenticity is everything." There's a significant anti-establishment undertone to our brand preference point-of-view, and we like to think that we have a strong ability to sense inauthenticity in a product or how it is marketed.

We like brands that ask for our feedback and perspective and that give us roles such as "ambassador" or "advisor," and the special notifications and access to new products that come with such status. We expect advertising and promotional materials to entertain us and look like us in all our diversity. Videos are the best way to reach us. We hate clothing or products featuring conspicuous logos and would much rather rock an outfit from a thrift store.

We ask — how can your product make the world a better place? We value brands that are ethical, sustainable, and that stand for values that align with our own. We especially connect to brands such as Toms that make giving back a part of their business plan and brand story. Toms made its mark by supporting a social good, giving away one pair of shoes for every one they sold. We're OK if a brand encourages consumption, as long as there's an element of social consciousness and corporate responsibility associated with the brand — think Nike, Everlane, and Levis. We know that we can achieve more than our age predicts and we crave brands that help us feel cool, cutting edge . . . and older — brands that don't define us, but allow us to define ourselves.

Given these three truths, I have three suggestions for how companies can pull together the different strands described above and connect with Gen Z. First, keep it natural. With school, extra-curriculars, part-time jobs, and social lives, Gen Z consumes a lot of information on a daily basis. To get anything to stick, brands have to be sneaky and thoughtful. You should pepper us with advertising that feels native and natural, inspirational and aspirational, placing products and concepts in pop culture, social media, video games, TV, and even educational materials.

Second, build a meaningful personal connection with us. Connect with our sense of adventure like Sperry Top Sider did with its Odysseys await campaign or connect with our desire for customization like Converse did with its "Made for You" concept. As Kayla Green of Saatchi & Saatchi suggests, give Gen Z some extra data on our phones if we spend some time with your product. Encourage us to post pictures of ourselves with your product on social media and comment or like our posts back. Engage with us directly, giving us challenges and tasks. Find ways to tailor your messages directly to us.

Finally, make it easy. We have a short attention span. Make everything concise, informative, and entertaining, able to compete with a 10-second Snapchat picture or a photo on Instagram. Make it easy to order online, make shops simple and approachable, make experiences smooth and streamlined.

There is no magic way to connect to Gen Z, but the insights above provide direction. Keep it simple, make it personal, and be authentic.

Connecting to Gen Z Profile: Britt Masback

I love my brother. He's very different from me, but I admire his passion for sports, interest in politics, and easy-going nature. Disturbed by what he saw in the American political landscape, he decided to volunteer for Hillary Clinton. He went door-to-door and made phone calls to primary voters across the country. Last summer, he attended the Democratic National Convention in Philadelphia, texting from the arena during many of the speeches about the power of the messages being conveyed. He's a high school freshman, right in the sweet spot of companies seeking to connect to Gen Z.

Do you consider yourself the "average" Gen Z consumer?

I'm not a huge shopper, but I am like most of my friends in that I spend a lot of time looking at my smartphone. I'm probably not as engaged by social media as some of my friends – I'm not big on Snapchat and I only occasionally add a photo to my Instagram account.

What are some of your favorite brands?

I'm a big fan of Nike – I like Nike's products, particularly their running products, soccer products, and some of their sportswear looks. I am very interested in politics so some of favorite brands are in the media space – *The Daily Show* and *Huffington Post*. I also like my sister's newsite, *WANT*.

What attracts you to a brand?

In the case of Nike, it is a combination of multiple things. I'm using many of the products for sports, so the functionality of the products is important to me. Next, the look of the product definitely matters, and I'm impressed by how Nike constantly refreshes the look of what are pretty straightforward products. I have a positive view of Nike and what it stands for, so I'm OK with wearing their logo, though I don't like Nike apparel with a giant logo. Lastly, it does matter for me that Nike sponsors some of the world's best athletes and teams.

What's the best way for a brand to maintain a connection with you?

I don't want to say that I'm lazy, but the more a brand can reach out to me with interesting and relevant information, the better. I don't hesitate to sign up for notifications from brands I like – I don't consider what they send me to be spam. I like receiving a heads up about Nike's latest running shoe or notification from *Huffington Post* of a new article on a subject of interest to me.

You've supported Hillary Clinton for president, how is she doing at connecting to younger voters?

It's been a tough year for her as she's battled Bernie Sanders during the primary season and now is battling apathy among Millennials and first-time Gen Z voters. I'm a Hillary fan, but I can also see reluctance by some younger voters to sign on to what appears to be a continuation of the status quo. I made a number of small contributions to Hillary's campaign, and hoped to get one of the "women's cards" that her campaign was sending to donors. It bothered me a bit that I never received the card after I made my donation.

Where do you see marketing to Gen Z going in the future?

The best way to market to my friends and me is to be where we spend our time – on Fantasy Football sites, on teen-oriented newsites (maybe not for everyone, but for me), on YouTube channels that we frequent, and via sponsorship of athletes we like. At some point, I'll become more of an active consumer. When it comes to buying things, the one thing I definitely care about are consumer reviews of products that interest me.

Chapter 10

Conclusion

How Identifying a Life Worth Living will help Gen Z become America's Greatest Generation

"HI, I'M GRACE MASBACK," I began. "And....I was an excellent sheep." The 12-step-like confession elicited shocked stares from the parents crowded into the chemistry classroom on back-to-school night. The head of school stood to my left, the high school principal to my right. I changed the slide on our carefully crafted Powerpoint, pausing for effect. I had their attention.

My journey to this moment began a year earlier, sparked by the words of William Deresiewicz, a former Yale professor. When he came to speak at my high school Deresiewicz derided American higher education and ridiculed my generation. He called us "mindless robots simply achieving for the point of achieving, lacking a clear life goal, purpose, or meaning." He had added, "You are all excellent sheep."

I reacted with visceral anger, resenting being classified and lampooned so cavalierly. Yet, as I brooded, his point began to resonate. What motivated me to do the things I did? Why did I sacrifice time for sleep, family, and friends for success and accomplishment? Did my goals and ambitions have meaning? I realized that I had never stopped to think about how my various activities, achievements, and desires fit with my vision of a meaningful life. I knew the same was true of many of my peers. Deresiewiez was right. Brooding segued to disgruntlement. I felt lost.

Weeks later, while visiting relatives on the East coast, I broached the topic of "excellent sheep" syndrome with my uncle, a minister. He responded by telling me about an undergraduate course at Yale University called "Life Worth Living" that harkened back to the original purpose of university education — facilitating conversations that allow students to understand how to live a life "worth living." The course examined history's great religious and secular works, evaluating claims about what makes for a meaningful life. Students could then apply those claims to their own lives.

It seemed I had found my antidote. Highly motivated, I contacted two of the Yale professors from the Yale Center For Faith & Culture who taught the course, Ryan McAnnally-Linz and Matthew Croasmun, and asked about its origins and objectives. As they described the course, they said their vision was to take it to other colleges. "Can I take it to my high school?" I asked. Somewhat dumbfounded by my aggressiveness, they chuckled and then agreed, offering me an internship aimed at translating the college course for high school consumption.

When I returned home, I went straight to my head of school, describing my personal journey and my proposal for the course. He agreed to sponsor the course and help to teach it, engaging the high school principal and dean of students as co-teachers. The year-long seminar would be offered only to seniors with the hope that we could help them find life's meaning prior to departing for the next chapter in their lives. Half the senior class signed up, but we only had 19 spots available.

I spent much of the summer that followed working with both Yale and my school to develop the course. In order to create the syllabus, I read the works of philosophers, religious figures, and scientists and structured class periods that featured discussions, guest speakers, service work, and experiential learning. This work required deep personal reflection. For the first time, I examined my actions and activities through the lens of whether they were helping me build a meaningful life. I abruptly stopped doing things that I'd been doing for no discernable purpose. I recognize that the process of reflection will take time, but I'm on my way.

Back in front of the parents, I smile and tell them how the course originated and how it would differ from other courses. I describe to them the transformative effect of the readings and reflections we will undertake. I end with a simple promise, "I discovered the antidote for the excellent sheep syndrome, and from now until May we'll be working with your kids to distill the essence of a life well lived."

I tell this story because the ultimate success of Gen Z in its unannounced, unacknowledged quest to become America's next "Greatest Generation" depends on Gen Z putting its life goals and day-to-day activities in perspective. While some people find that perspective through organized religion and others emerge perfectly well-balanced due to idyllic parental upbringing, the vast majority of us travel through life without a defined purpose, struggling to make sense of our hopes, dreams, desires, ambitions, and sense of responsibility to family, community, and the future.

As the high school analog of the Yale "Life Worth Living" class is a pilot program for 19 students in the Pacific Northwest, we can't count on it changing the course of history for Gen Z. But we can closely watch the outcome of that experiment and others going on at schools and within community-based organizations across the country to determine how best to mold not just the best and brightest of the generation, but the generation as a whole, so as to help it realize its lofty potential.

Matching the societal contribution of what newscaster Tom Brokaw termed "The Greatest Generation" won't be easy. That generation had its formative years during the Great Depression, went on to lead the fight for freedom during World War II, and then helped spur global rebuilding that fueled groundbreaking societal progress. It wasn't a generation that struggled and fought for fame and fortune, but because of a deep sense of duty . . . a sense that it was "the right thing to do."

Brokaw's description of the "The Greatest Generation" is compelling. As Franklin Delano Roosevelt said about them at the time, "This generation of Americans has a rendezvous with destiny." It was their destiny to be born during the Roaring 20s, come of age during the deprivation of the Great Depression, and put their lives on hold and on the line when they headed into battle against the Axis Empire or took on gender-bending roles never before granted to women. In Brokaw's words, everyone had "a sense of purpose" that connected our country in a way never seen before. Their contributions and leadership extended well beyond the war.

It is my sincere hope that Gen Z is challenged neither by a Great Depression nor a World War. I am hopeful that we can prove ourselves and make a dramatic contribution to society in ways fundamentally different from the previous Greatest Generation. I like our chances. Gen Z is battling through the same issues as every generation that came before us, but we are far more independent, have more power, and can control our lives better than any previous generation. And, call it the arrogance of youth, but Gen Z remains optimistic even while living through the onslaught of negativity that surrounds us today. We look for the bright side and embrace it.

While most of the world thinks things are getting worse, there are many reasons for hope, and Gen Z embraces that outlook. I get it – it's easy to be pessimistic – we are bombarded with negative news about natural disasters and human disasters of every kind. Things that might have merited a few column inches in a newspaper or a *Life Magazine* photo spread in the 1960s are projected directly to our homes and handheld devices in living color. It's impossible to ignore the graphic nature of the pain and suffering of others, and the stories come with relentless regularity.

We remain upbeat, looking for positive evidence. Recently, the *Economist* reviewed Johan Norberg's excellent book, *Progress: Ten Reasons to Look Forward to the Future*, highlighting some random examples of progress — global poverty has fallen in half, 68 percent of the world has modern sanitation (up from 24 percent in 1980), and the average IQ of Americans has risen from 100 to 118 over the past 50 years. Or, as Nicholas Kristof reported in a recent column, for most of human history, the majority of humans were illiterate. Today, more than 85 percent of the world's adults are literate.

To Gen Z, this good news represents our building blocks for a positive and successful future. Consumed and motivated by our passions, we are ready to engineer a better world. The engineering analogy is apposite. Our engagement with the world is not a passive engagement, but one that involves taking our passions and talents and figuring out how we can design and build our most effective form of contribution.

Gen Z's connection, to one another and to the world, is truly global in nature. This grows out of our unprecedented access to education and the fact that our parents have engaged in a global competition to give us the best education in the world. Who would have thought twenty or fifty years ago that parents in London, or Mumbai, or Stockholm, or Minneapolis would be obsessed with how students in Shanghai or Singapore were performing on language and math exams, but that has been our middle school and high school reality. The downside of the drive for a better education is that we've had more homework and higher expectations than any previous generation. The upside is that we've been provided groundbreaking instruction and incredible access to classes like Life Worth Living and Hybrid Identities and programs like Start-up Weekend.

Part of that education, inside and outside of the classroom, has been our unprecedented access to and education in technology. Being tech natives enables us to establish and nurture the unique connections that allow us to work with and learn from (and teach) the very Chinese students with whom our parents wanted us to compete, and it is a two-way sharing of information, culture, and capability. I will never be as good a math student as my friend from Shanghai, but he is mystified by my fearlessness as a writer and my creativity as an entrepreneur. We are only seeing a mere inkling of the power of these global connections and technological aptitudes of Gen Z, so the best is yet to come.

One reason that I'm so bullish on the future is that Gen Z has already proven it is a self-directed and highly productive generation. Scarred by the fear we saw in our parents and the Millennials just ahead of us as they struggled with the Great Recession, we are careful, particularly with money, but focused on pushing ourselves to be efficient in everything we do, maximizing the outcome from whatever energy we expend. OK, I admit it – we are a bit nervous about student debt, what the job prospects will be when we start emerging from college in the early 2020s, and what the state of the world will be in our future, but we give ourselves comfort by playing an active role in addressing all the things that worry us.

Our entrepreneurial spirit helps us assuage our concerns about financial and job matters. Given that we are already comfortable with the idea of starting our own business (or working with a friend who is starting one), we can reduce our anxiety about whether there will be a job waiting for us or how we will handle a giant loan burden. That same entrepreneurial spirit is what gives me confidence that we can make an historic contribution to society. We face problems with the same can-do spirit that the previous "Greatest Generation" faced in World War II and its aftermath. Like that generation, Gen Z's solutions to problems already in existence and those to come will be identified by our creativity and achieved by our grit and determination.

We'll achieve all this with an unprecedented focus on "community," whether it means our immediate friend circle, the place where we live, our country, or the world. We are already proving that we can deliver three great things to our communities – our commitment to being a positive force, our ability to ideate creative solutions to vexing problems, and our willingness to work to make things happen. This is not a passing fancy but is an attribute hard-wired into the makeup of Gen Z.

The path toward making contributions to our community is smoothed by our non-partisan and w approach. Yes, it feels as if it will take a miracle to yank our country out of the partisan quagmire in which it finds itself, but think how gridlocked with frustration and inaction the American political scene has been during our entire existence. We've endured boot camp like training via the media in what doesn't work and have had plenty of experience at our micro level with what does work. Our tolerance and the post-race, post-gender mindset of Gen Z are partially a product of the gigantic demographic shift in the make-up of our generation and partially the fruit of our seeing so clearly the failures of partisanship and intolerance.

I end where I began, with the admission that this book is biased – biased in favor of a super-positive view of my generation and biased in favor of my predicted outcomes for my generation as it matures and takes on its leadership role in society. Even if I'm wrong because I've over-extrapolated the experiences I've had and/or the research I've done to draw certain conclusions, no one can deny the power of this "next" generation, by virtue of its size (and the economic implications that grow out of that), its diversity, its tech savvy, and its potential for impact. No matter what, it's guaranteed to be an exciting ride!

Life worth living profile: Sydney Palmer

Sydney Palmer is a 17-year-old high school senior from Portland, Oregon. She is actively engaged in a variety of community activities in an around Portland and was also a Co-Founder of WANT. She is one of the leaders of her school's service learning organization, CommuniCare, and works at Mercy Corps Portland as a filmmaker-in- residence. When Sydney is in not in school, she is an avid outdoors person, hiking through Eastern Oregon, leading her school's rock climbing club, and taking pictures and videos of the natural world around her. She is confidently designed-minded and plans to pursue a career in architecture and design.

Many people say that our generation is a generation of "excellent sheep" — that we are achieving for the point of achieving. Do you agree?

I think for many of us the increasing competitiveness of

college admission and the illusion that going to the "right" college will lead to the "right" job has created the mirage of a tried and true path to success. We see it shimmering in the distance, the Ivy League sweatshirts, the high-profile internships, the glowing praises of superiors. But, what's lacking for many is any true passion. It should be said that there is nothing inherently wrong with this path, but too often it is championed as the end for everyone, and it's used as a gold standard to which all other paths are compared unfavorably. I think any achievement without some underlying connection to an individual's passion leads them down a path of emptiness.

Is it important to have meaning behind what you do? If so, why?

Absolutely. After school ends, people no longer have the guardrails of school to structure their progress. If you lack any kind of internal motivation and meaning it will lead to misdirection and stagnation in life after college.

What have you done to identify meaning within your own life?

I have nurtured passions and curiosities in my life and tried to work out a reasonable way to pursue these interests in my higher education and eventual job prospects.

In what areas do you continue to struggle?

I feel a lot of shame when comparing myself to my peers at school in terms of college plans and academics. I feel like I should and could have been doing more, better, and earlier, like there is some expectation that I haven't met. I would hazard a guess that many of my peers feel similarly, which pop culture references as FOMO, fear of missing out. But, it's not beach vacations we lust after, rather it's some opaque notion of "success." What does success mean — money, power, fame? None of us are quite sure, but regardless many blindly strive for that 4.0 GPA or that Ivy League acceptance letter. And, when I reflect, I certainly fall short of these societal markers of perceived success in high school, yet now recognize that I never wanted those indicia for the right reasons. I wanted to attend certain schools for personal and social validation rather than as tools to pursue something I cared deeply about. I feel better recognizing all of that.

What do you think needs to happen to encourage more young people to find meaning in what they do? How will both society and culture need to change?

My peers and I need to ground our drive in passion rather than in fear of falling short of expectations, either ours or society's. Diving into a topic or field of pursuit that an individual finds personal meaning in, completely (or significantly) disregarding the opinions and judgments of friends, parents and strangers is a must. Honestly, I think the arbitrary pursuit of "success" boils down to the same energy that keeps social media afloat, the need to show off. We want to Instagram that Bali beachfront photo to grab the attention of our "friends" on social media and in the same way we wish for our peers and their friends to whisper, "Wow, she got into Stanford." Of course, prestigious college institutions can hardly be held responsible for a widespread social phenomena, but the general American student body needs to see that these places are ultimately just a name on a sweatshirt that you won't wear all-that-often (or, even worse, a bumper sticker on your parents' car). The real truth is that your education is what you make of it. If following your passion leads you to a top university, then you will likely excel there and afterwards. However, without that childlike curiosity and innate energy for something of meaning, even if you crafted the perfect application and have engineered your extra curriculars since 8th grade to achieve the holy grail of admissions, at the end of your four years you will end up holding nothing more than that $300,000 sweatshirt.

What goals do you have for the future?

To get into an architecture program in college that will challenge and inspire me. To enjoy my passions of climbing and backpacking to the fullest extent I can while living a life balanced with my work/school/family.